A DESTINY OF MEMORIES

BOOK I: FIRE AND RAIN

D. RAMATI

BLACK ROSE
writing™

ISBN: 978-1-61296-718-9
PUBLISHED BY BLACK ROSE WRITING
www.blackrosewriting.com

Printed in the United States of America
Suggested retail price $15.95

A Destiny of Memories is printed in Constantia

To a generation who checked out of Vietnam but never left.

A DESTINY OF

MEMORIES

He stood on a cold, grey, January's shore...and
As he finally stopped running,
he felt that somehow he had been completely
And utterly...betrayed.

CHAPTER 1

Everybody walks in the twilight of sanity at some time in their life, when forces beyond their control shape and mold the fabric of reality, bending the wills of small and unimportant people into accepting the abstract political goals and desires of the ruling few. There have always been men caught up in this dehumanizing process...trapped somewhere between opposing realities of life and death, truth and lies, light and dark. He was one of them.

There was nothing special about him, except maybe his unique serial number, USMC 2201072.

He was on his way home from months of combat in Vietnam. Like tens of thousands of his generation, he agreed to fight a far-away war for idealistic reasons; sent to fight a war to save a poor and downtrodden people from the evils of Communism, and to defend America. Now, after the reality of war had fully set in, the fire of idealism and patriotism had burned down to the glowing embers of a determination simply to survive.

Only 36 hours ago, he was at an insignificant dusty hellhole in Vietnam, and now he was circling O'Hare airport, Chicago, the city of his birth, where twenty years earlier everything began for him on a stormy summer evening when he was born in Southside Memorial Hospital, in 1947. Like many children born before the age of modern medicine, he was a born healthy but quickly contracted jaundice; refusing to eat or respond to any treatment. His body quickly became emaciated.

As the days passed, and he continued to lose weight, the doctors gave up hope for his survival. His very Catholic Aunt had him baptized by a priest, last rites were administered, and in retaliation his mother, who was not what could be called a religious person, demanded that he be circumcised in remembrance of their father, Eli who was an assimilated Jew. The circumcision was done by a Jewish doctor at her request and he was given his Hebrew Name: David.

To everyone's surprise, after the circumcision, his condition improved. He began to eat, and gain weight. Even though mother named him David, his baptismal name was written on the birth certificate: Timothy. In Vietnam, his nom de guerre soon became "Brad".

Being circumcised was very unusual for a gentile born in the 40's, but it would have an impact on his future life, specifically when he went into the Marines where he was asked about his religion in the receiving barracks at Marine Corps boot camp. He thought for a minute and then answered, "Agnostic?". The clerk looked at him, frowned and then asked, "Are you circumcised?" He said he was and the clerk seemed visibly happy at not having to write down a word he probably couldn't spell, and so wrote "Jewish" in the service record book then punched Jewish on his aluminum dog tags; aluminum rectangles that he would carry with him for years.

The year 1947 was also the same year that Al Capone died, and the year that Jackie Robinson made history: Jackie Robinson changed everything for black Chicagoans and possibly set the stage for the struggle that lay ahead for his people. This was a year before the military integrated, seven years before Brown v. Board of Education, and eight years before Rosa Parks refused to step to the rear of a Montgomery bus. Jackie Robinson wasn't just nudging people out of their comfort zones; he was shoving them with both hands. Over 46,000 people came to Wrigley Field that warm May day in 1947 to see the Dodgers vs. Cubs game. Never before had a black man stepped on a Chicago field to play big league-ball. Some of his Dodger teammates initially refused to take the field with him, and among the Cubs as well, there was talk of a boycott. But when he took the field for his debut game in the Major Leagues, the people clapped and cheered. The Dodgers won, 4-2. When the game ended, black Chicago fans climbed on the roof of the Dodgers' team bus and leaned into its windows, trying to steal one more look at Robinson, the man who crossed the line.

He had served with blacks in Vietnam. Some were heroes, others were not, but all lived or died as United States Marines, and they were forever his brothers. The Marines only recognized one color, Marine Corps Green.

Now, twenty years after Robinson broke the mold, he sat in a window seat, still smelling of Vietnam. No amount of washings would ever get rid of the faint smell of death, gunpowder, and napalm, which was both a physical and spiritual stench. It was unusual for a Marine to be going home in ill-fitting civilian dress, and under normal circumstance, he would be in a freshly pressed uniform, but the emergency orders that had pulled him out of the 'Nam left no time for spit and polish. He had a short layover in Seattle where a Good Samaritan had given him some extra clothing, which allowed him to change from his jungle utilities, to ill-fitting jeans and a short-sleeved shirt too large for his shrunken frame. Those battered jungle utilities had been more a part of him than was the city below with its sleeping hundreds of thousands; a city both unaware and uncaring that yet another Marine was coming back from hell. The "lucky ones" would return, but unfortunately, the memories of Vietnam would stay with them forever.

For more hours than he could count, he had been fighting to stay awake, but kept drowsing into a limbo, which was both part dream and also part memory. He dozed for a moment and then snapped awake as he felt cold waves of fear fueling his body with a rush of adrenalin; causing him to react automatically with the instincts developed in Vietnam...instantly wary and alert. He had learned on patrol to be suspicious of anything different; anything even slightly out of place and here, in "The World", everything was out of place, and his fear and caution made him as dangerous as he would be on patrol.

He felt naked without his rifle. How could he defend himself? The adrenaline rushes continued, and after each attack subsided, he clung to the reality that he was home now. This was the United States. He was back in The World. There were no enemies here. Nevertheless, even here, a part of his mind and soul remained in Vietnam, ten thousand miles away, where even in the insanity of war, there yet remained a familiarity of belonging to something that he desperately refused to let go. Only now, he realized for the first time what his old gunnery sergeant had told him was stark truth and reality; 'you can take the Marine out of Vietnam, but you can never take Vietnam out of the Marine'.

As he saw his reflection in the port window, the memories reached out and held him like a jealous lover and when everything dissolved into other scenes, he closed his eyes and slipped back into the familiar and brutally beautiful landscapes of Vietnam.

. . .

"You're goin' home, Corporal!" The words hit him like a bucket of cold water. He savored the words and let them sink into his conscience until they took on the form of an irrefutable fact. This is the day for which he had waited and fought to survive. His orders back to The World were in, marking an end to months of continuous combat. He had survived...and was going home to The World!

"Yeah Gunny, back to The World! I'm so short that snakes shit on me." The Gunny's face was an open book filled with Marine Corps history. A story etched in flesh that told of World War II, the Pacific Islands, then Korea, and now Vietnam...the Gunny was a "lifer" whose eyes had seen the horrors of three wars; his sanity preserved by a life dedicated to Corps and Country. No matter how far apart they were in age and rank, he felt a kinship with the Gunny. As chance would have it, the Gunny had served in the same unit with his two Uncles; on islands that no Marine would ever forget: Guadalcanal and Iwo Jima. In the Corps that was as good as, or better than, being family.

"Brad, when you get back to the states don't forget to send me a bottle of Jack Daniel's Green Label. And never forget; no one ever really leaves Vietnam." His nickname in Vietnam was "Brad," a name that would stick with him for the duration.

"No sweat, Gunny, it's on the top of my list." He slung his M-14 rifle over his shoulder and picked up a small kit bag that contained essentials for the trip home, paused a moment to look back at the Tom O'Shea, a 105-mm Howitzer that belonged to a crew of Irish Marines and then started walking for the helicopter landing zone, or the LZ as they called it. He had been a part of that gun crew once, before volunteering to go out as a Forward Scout-Observer (FO).

That gun had seen a lot of action, and the years and the wars had taken its toll. No one knew who was older, the Gunnery Sergeant, or the Tom O'Shea. A lot of the equipment the Marines were using was left over from the Korean War, and some of it was even WWII vintage. The

Marine Corps, always first to serve and last to receive a budget from the Defense Department, had to beg, borrow, or steal its equipment. Still, what the Marines lacked in equipment they more than made up for in raw courage.

It was summer, and, with the monsoon still a month away, everything was covered with a fine powder of red dust. Each step he took caused the dust to ripple outward from his boots like miniature waves of blood stained water. It was as if he were wading in some surreal stream. Summer in the "I Corps" was an unchanging and relentless dry heat that burned the soul as well as the body—just as unbearable in its own way as the cold never-ending rains of the monsoon were during the long hell of the Vietnamese winter. They had seen fire and they had seen rain. The I Corps Tactical Zone (pronounced 'eye corps') was bordered by the South China Sea on the East and Laos on the West. In the North, it was the first line of defense against the North Vietnamese Army (NVA). This was 3rd Marine Division Country.

The summer sun blazed down like a vengeful Mayan god gazing accusingly from a crystal blue cloudless sky. He could almost hear the heat thermals rumble as they stirred up miniature dust devils that swirled angrily through the fire base, causing wave after wave of dust the color of dried blood to splash against the sandbagged emplacements. 'Surf's up' he thought, smiling at his own black humor as the weight of this world; his world, bore down causing him to sink ever deeper into the red dust.

His body ached from months of hardship and was tired beyond caring. He was down from 190 pounds to an emaciated 125, and he knew that this fatigue was not caused by semi-starvation; rather it was more akin to the prolonged agony of the long distance runner...a pain that came from someplace deep inside where some people believe the soul resides; a centrally located throb; an emptiness always being filled with a profound sorrow for friends who, torn by the raging beasts of war, were now memories, soon to become the bad dreams, which would haunt him forever. 'Pain, abhors a vacuum,' he thought.

The helipad LZ (helicopter landing zone) was the highest feature of this surreal landscape, situated on a small mound-like hill, it was their lifeline; the single road that ran the entire length of Vietnam was cut more times than not, leaving a tenuous resupply route by air as the only viable alternative. The heat distorted the road's image causing it to dance seductively from left to right, and then alternately, changing shape like the fun-house mirrored reflections which had entertained him and his friends in a childhood that belonged to an America built on the culture created by Walt Disney Studios, and John Wayne movies; a culture that had seduced them into volunteering for a tour in hell.

This mirage was appropriate to "their Vietnam"; a huge senseless psychedelic joke being played on anyone luckless enough to be caught within. They had long since stopped fighting for the right of the Vietnamese to "self-determination" having replaced that with a much simpler credo: do whatever it takes to survive and, "Kill 'em first and let God sort them out."

Growing up in the years of the Cuban Missile Crises, and the "do not ask what your country can do for you" euphoria of President Kennedy, had made his volunteering for duty with the Marines in Vietnam an inevitability, a duty that had inexorably destroyed all that had gone before. He was something like 13 or 14 years old, standing in awe and watching the newly mobilized hometown members 32nd National Guard Infantry Division as they marched to the trucks, which would transport them to staging points in response to the Communist threat from Cuba. Filled with uninhibited patriotism he had wanted to march off with them and now, years later that wish had come true as he was sent to fight yet another Communist threat, except that this time the threat had gone on far too long. No one had told them to "be careful what you wish for" and had "They" done so, he probably wouldn't have listened.

"Just live one day at a time, Tim," his Uncle Donald had advised when he joined up. Yet every day that went by allowed Vietnam to turn the survivors into a generation of hedonists, incapable of feeling anything except a tremendous drive to return to that elusive paradise of memories always referred to as The World.

They expected the American people to be grateful. They expected them to remember them—to mourn their dead, and welcome the lucky ones, the battered survivors, back into the ranks of the living. The thought of going home filled his mind with visions of unending cold drinks, fast food, girls, and being accepted back into the community and the home for which he had been so willing to lay down his life. He had done his best to help North Vietnamese soldiers die for their country, and while feeling no satisfaction at the thought, he wasn't particularly bothered by it either. The idea of taking life had become commonplace and acceptable to everyone. The ghosts of the daily kills he participated in had yet to appear in his dreams—or haunt the periphery of his vision when, in the still quiet times, he would sit alone in a very private darkness.

He passed a group of Marines, their new utilities betraying the fact that they were 'boot[1] to the 'Nam'. 'Replacements!' he thought, 'Fresh meat for the grinder!' He looked down at his own jungle utilities, faded and torn, scrounged out of a pile of clothing and equipment that had been taken from the dead and wounded marines, some of it was blood stained. It was fair game for 'scrounging'[2] and marines would pick over the pile for usable jackets, pants, and jungle boots.

Looking at these new fish, he wondered how fast a young man could age in Vietnam. There was a huge generation gap even though they were all about the same age. They annoyed him. What were they doing here, in his Vietnam? These fresh faced hard-charging young Marines, ready to kill—ready to die—were just more fresh meat. 'Stupid fish', he thought, 'already on the hook and don't even know it.'

He knew them very well because they were he and his friends, the grateful dead, who not so very long ago had arrived from an imaginary world now so far away; a world that had rapidly receded in both space and time as the agent orange poisoned jungles and forests of Vietnam claimed either their lives or their souls. They all wanted to kill. That was what they were trained to do, and what was expected of them. Looking them over, he couldn't help wondering how many would die, who would be maimed, and who would make it home. Replacements could never

---

[1] Boot: Boot Camp: One who is just starting his service.

[2] Scrounging: Noun: Scrounger. How Marines got extra equipment and rations and a Scrounger was held in high esteem for his ability to provide the needed equipment.

take the place his friends.

One of them got up, smiled in a way that reminded him of a puppy wanting to make friends, and began walking toward him and for a second, he flashed back in time and saw himself as a new replacement, looking at the veteran marines on their way back home. The circle closes, he thought, and turning his back on them, he entered the C.P. (Command Post).

Inside were the tired old men of thirty and forty years who ran this small part of hell. Like their Viet Cong (V.C.) and North Vietnamese Army (NVA) counterparts in the hills, they were more concerned with the tomorrows than the todays. Today was past history almost as soon as it happened. Men died, were maimed, destroyed both mentally and morally, but tomorrow the war would be won...and these men, the lords of hell, would go on to their promotions. 'Lifers', he thought, and walked over to the battalion Executive Officer (XO), "Corporal Bratvold, reporting as ordered Sir."

"Bratvold?" the X.O glanced up with tired indifference, "yeah...they're cutting your orders right now Brad...wait outside. We'll call you when they're ready."

He turned and walked outside. No salutes in the 'Nam, saluting a superior officer would let a sniper know who to put on the top of his kill list. Lighting a cigarette he slumped against the sandbag wall of the C.P. and talked to the replacements waiting to see the 'old man'. "What outfit did you draw?"

"Hotel Company."

"I drew Golf," another replacement joined in.

"Doesn't matter much," he said, "they're both good outfits."

On the demilitarized zone, referred to only as "The Z", there were daily artillery duels, bringing incoming death, night Patrols, search and destroy missions, whatever it took, and it was all the same no matter with which unit you served. Everything was a matter of luck or divine intervention. Most of his friends were already statistics. Seven hundred and fifty officers and men of the original battalion had already gone home before him...some of them in body bags, others returned to their families as cripples and some with no physical marks at all, finishing their tour in the 'Nam but having the 'look'; eyes of old men, staring out of the faces of boys not old enough to vote or be served in a bar; boys who became men in Vietnam—men old enough to kill and to die.

On his last operation, they were caught in the open. The N.V.A. had withdrawn under fire, and the battalion had charged, marine-style, into the valley. It was a trap. The battalion was caught in a box barrage of white phosphorous; fire raining from the sky that made napalm look like a mercy killing. 'Yes, they'd seen fire and they'd seen rain'. Then from across the 'Z' the enemy counter-attacked...a division of N.V.A. regulars. The fight went on for three days, until as they were being overrun Biff had called artillery fire on their own positions. That was the only thing that stopped the NVA. The pictures kept flashing through his mind...Murf, the radio operator, Lt. Biff Mullins and what was left of the rest of their FO team, being evacuated...stacked and lashed down to the tanks that had finally arrived.

The pictures of that operation in Con Tien had made the evening news. People watched without understanding as a tank stacked with the dead moved past the CBS camera crew. He remembered seeing an arm jarred into a semblance of life by the moving tank, its hand seeming to move in a bizarre farewell wave...set in motion by the lurching tank that carried it, waving goodbye—waving goodbye to the past, to what they were and what they had become, and as he watched the tanks take his friends to graves registration the thought flashed through his mind like a silent litigant asking again and again, 'Why you still alive, Brad? You should be there with them, those honored dead...the grateful dead, now in the underworld, where there is no wind, and the chariot of the sun is towed along, towed by the grateful dead.'

"What's it like over here Corporal?" the question brought him out of his dark thoughts and yet it took a long time until he finally answered, "The place grows on you," he smiled at this private joke and thought about the fungus growing between his toes.

"Brad!" The battalion clerk stuck his head out of the C.P.

"Yeah." he answered, grateful to be able to escape the dead men walking.

"The Major'll see ya now."

He walked inside and stood in front of the Major's desk. The Major was a career office, Annapolis, football hero, square faced and tall, "Sit down, Brad," he sat and waited for the next move. The Major was using his 'command' voice. "They zapped Biff." The major folded his hands, as if he were praying.

"Yes sir, Biff was the officer in charge of our F.O. team. When the gooks[3] over-ran us he called in fire on our own position."

"I'm recommending him for a Navy Cross. There should be something in this for you too. I understand that you're the lone survivor of the team."

"Yes sir." 'Shove the medals up your ass,' he thought.

"How come you made it?" Had the major just accused him of having committed a crime?

"Just damn lucky, sir," he said. 'Why had he survived?' he remembered the concussion of the incoming high explosive 155mm artillery rounds and losing consciousness until he rejoined the world with a terrific headache and a ringing in his ears as a corpsman was busily slapping a pressure bandage on his head. Evidently, the N.V.A. had left him for dead.

"That makes three times you've been hit this year, son, that's a Purple Heart with a Wounds Cluster in your SRB (Service Record Book)."

The major seemed to think it was a record, but he considered the wounds to be no more than 'Band-Aid jobs' so he only answered, "Yes sir."

Thoughts about Biff came to mind; Biff, who had joined the team fresh from a Navy ROTC[4] program and after spending a few weeks at Staging Battalion[5] in California, was flown straight to Danang and from there over mean trails and days of fire and rain, to Dong Ha, ConThien, and on to KheSahn. He was idealistic, trying to be a friend to his men

---

[3] GOOK: The earliest recorded uses of this term were by U.S. Marines when referring to Haitians and Filipinos. It continued to be common slang in the American military, especially during World War II, the Korean War, and the Vietnam War.

[4] The Reserve Officers' Training Corps (ROTC) is a college-based * Officer training program for training commissioned officers of the United States Armed Forces.

[5] Staging Battalion: United States. Marine Corps. Infantry Training Regiment. 2nd. United States. Marine Corps. Schools Battalion, United States Marine Corps.

instead of only being their officer. With Biff, there hadn't been that insurmountable distance usually found between a marine officer and the enlisted men.

He remembered Biff when they first met. For want of something better to do, the Commanding Officer (C.O.) had decided to hold a rifle inspection, and since Biff was the new officer, had put him in charge. They cleaned their weapons of several months' accumulated dust and resignedly formed a line for the inspection.

Biff had stopped in front of him and took his rifle, "Not very clean, Corporal, how does she shoot?"

"Shoots fine sir," 'Chicken shit second lieutenant', he thought. The Lieutenant passed down the line. After the inspection the company first sergeant chewed his ass and gave him the unwanted job of burning the 'shitters'; barrels cut in half with handles welded on...receptacles that sat under the two and four-holer latrines. They had to be removed, carried by a two-man team, and ignited, their contents burned and then returned. Later, when his work was finished Biff had stopped by, "I'm sorry I got you into trouble with the Top (the Sergeant Major). Your rifle was clean, but I felt that I had to find something wrong, to prove myself." The admission had startled him.

"That's OK, Lieutenant, so I pulled four hours of shit detail, so what." Actually, it was 'skating duty' with nothing more to do while the shit was burning than to smoke pot and bullshit with the rest of the shit detail.

"Well," Biff looked embarrassed, "the guys call you Brad, right? Look, I just wanted you to know. I'm not really chicken shit...just new to all this." Biff walked away.

The conversation had been totally unreal. Was an officer in the marines admitting to a mistake, apologizing, and even making an attempt at friendliness? This was someone who needed watching. Later, when they were fresh out of forward observers because of death and jungle rot, Biff had asked him to volunteer.

"Why should I volunteer?"

"Because, Brad, I can work with you and also because I think you'll be good at it," Biff said.

17

And, so he agreed to join the team. For the next few months, they had worked deep in the boonies[6] with a rifle company of the 2nd Battalion 4th Marines, then a few operations with the Third Recon, and back to the Fourth again. The days on Patrol and nights of sweating terror had passed in a daze until in the end; he was the last man standing of the original team.

"I think he'll get it," the voice of the Major brought him back.

"Sir?"

"The Navy Cross," the Major said, "I think that he'll get the Navy Cross."

"Be real nice for his family," he said, trying to keep the sarcasm out of his voice. Biff had taken R&R (Rest and Recreation) in Hawaii in order to get married just a month before he was killed.

"Anyway, here're your papers. And have a good time back in The World," as he took his orders the Major continued, "and come back in one piece, Brad. You'll have a new team to train next month when the replacement FOs arrive." His papers! The Golden Ring in the Merry-go-round! The first prize in the lottery! The Mother Lode! Papers to the states! Nevertheless, it had cost him.

He hadn't wanted to extend his tour in Vietnam, but the letters from home had been getting...strange...something had gone wrong with his mothers' new marriage. She was frightened, uncertain, and had begged him to come home as soon as possible. So he had to extend for another tour in order to get the thirty days 'basket leave'. He was going home, back to The World. What would await him after the thirty days leave when he had to return to hell wasn't important in light of the opportunity to go home.

First, he thought he would straighten things out at home, and then show off his medals to the small-town girls, enjoy being a hero, have drinks bought for him, and be generally fussed over, as was only right. There had been a demonstration against DOW chemical recruiters on the University, but that had happened long after he left for Vietnam, and had nothing whatsoever to do with the University from two years before—a University more concerned with football games and panty

---

6   The boonies: The middle of nowhere

raids than war protests. He kicked himself every day for leaving school and volunteering for the Marines and then compounding his idiocy, by volunteering for Vietnam.

Taking the papers, he had a premonition that they would never meet again. This immediately made him paranoid. Leaving the CP, he could feel the cross hairs of a telescopic sight focusing on the back of his head and braced himself for the impact...several tons of pressure exploding in a red mist of blood and gray matter, and later, the sound of the rifle drifting in from the perimeter—a sound which, mercifully, he would never hear. The only mercy in war was that you would never hear the shot that killed you. He'd seen it once before. A sergeant, his tour completed, was going up the ramp to a waiting cargo plane in Dong Ha; going back to The World, his papers in hand, joking and smiling, then suddenly, without a sound, splattered against the side of the plane, dead...and after another second, the sound of the 0.50 caliber sniper rifle...and everybody went down on their faces praying... 'please God, not me, let it be someone else'.

Everyone sweats in Vietnam, but he could feel a different kind of sweat, which trickled down the small of his back, as if death was playing with his spine; his mouth went dry...he didn't even care if he were a coward or not...had stopped caring many months before...then, miraculously, he could breathe again; Death had passed him by. The sniper hadn't fired...or perhaps there was no sniper.

As he continued walking toward the landing zone (L.Z), the feeling of being in the cross hairs receded as the reality that the journey home finally started to sink in. All he had to do was survive long enough to get to the LZ, board a huey gunship, fly south to Da Nang, and catch a bird to The World. He thought about the birds of home...the blue jays calling softly in the warm moist summer heat seeming to cry 'rain, rain'. There were no birds in Vietnam other than the birds of war and death; the gun ships, phantom attack jets, the B-52 bombers flying so high you never saw them and only felt the earth shake under your feet as they dropped their deadly eggs, and then, the nighttime visits of the Douglas AC-47 Spooky that was lovingly known by the Marines as 'Puff, the Magic Dragon'. When the shit hits the fan that blessed bestial howl was the last thing the enemy heard as Puff cut lose with its 7.62mm. G.E. mini-guns placing a round every 2 yards in any VC or NVA concentration. Puff was a godsend to marines fighting against the odds. Steams of dragon fire would come out of a big black silhouette, cutting branches, trees, grass, and anything living to shreds.

The L.Z. for the Hueys contained a primitive sandbagged control center run by a harassed PFC (Private First Class). The air controller's job, outside of staying alive, was to coordinate the flights of aircraft landing and taking off from his small empire. In this miniature Grand Central Station, you could catch a ride on any one of the many supply helicopters or special missions' birds that landed every five minutes or so to take off bodies, unload and load supplies, and take short-timers, like him, back to The World.

Sharing a trip with the full body bags already lined up in a neat row for shipment south didn't bother him 'Nothing mattered'...nothing but getting out. It was always the same...brown sandbags, radio antenna, machine gun emplacements, and the dusty weary ageless marines manning them...everything, incongruously silhouetted against a striking blue sky. Always the dust, red as blood, and the cloudless blue sky, unchanging until the monsoon, when all would be grey sky above, mud below.

"When's the next bird in." he asked the air controller.

"'Bout sixty minutes," he answered, "if you're going to Da Nang, that is. The next bird to Da Nang is comin' in real soon," he pointed to a stack of body bags, "gotta take them back 'afore they start stinking real bad. They're the boys from that ambush at the water-point last night. Real nasty...Charlie cut their balls off and put their pricks in their mouths."

He nodded, "Bastard Gooks!" The Marines had learned from the enemy, and no-holds barred and down and dirty were SOP (Standard operating procedure) for both sides now. 'Nice guys don't last long in the 'Nam'.

"Don't matter who I share the chopper with, so long as it's going my way. Nope, I'm not particular if the dead have balls or not."

"You must be going home. I know I wouldn't ride back with dead bodies for anything less than a ticket to The World."

"That's right. Got my ticket right here," he patted his shirt, "I'm getting the fuck out of this place and going back to the land of the big P.X."

"Well, good luck to you...hey, call my folks will you, tell them the last time you saw me I was still alive."

"Sure," he lied...'fuck you too' he thought, 'best way to get zapped is to ask someone to tell your parents you are still alive.', "just write it down and I'll give 'em a call," he said aloud.

He heard a low rumbling coming from the rolling hills to the South. A thick black column of smoke began to snake its almost perfectly vertical way into the unforgiving sky.

"That'll be the morning convoy out of Phu Bai. Looks like no mail today either. Another ambush," the air controller spat a long thin brown streak of tobacco, "care for a 'chaw?"

He shook his head, "No thanks," he sat back and watched the pillar of smoke. Back in Boot Camp, they had taken the two-year draftees aside and, after assuring them that they were all going to be sent to the infantry to die, offered them a way out; if they agreed to enlist for another year they would be sent to truck-driving school. Faced with the choice of drive or die, they agreed, signed up for another year, and spent the next thirteen months on convoy duty in Vietnam, where the best they could hope for was coming home as an amputee. The sandbagged floor of the trucks was supposed to keep their balls intact, but it didn't do much for their feet.

Someone limped up and sat beside him, "any birds going out?"

"He says there's one comin' in another hour."

"How long you been back from Con Tien?" Both of them had been there. It was something in the eyes and the red dust that covered them like a semi-transparent second skin so he didn't ask how the guy knew.

"Not long," he answered, then noticing the marine's bandaged arm he asked, what happened to the wing?"

"This?" the man pated his bandage, "bobby trap, an arrow, it went clear through and had to break the tip off and pull the rest back out. I hope it will be enough to get me some time at a base hospital and to keep me out of the boonies for a while. Doesn't even hurt much since they gave me a shot of morphine but the arm still smells like shit."

"Cigarette?" he offered.

"Thanks. Light it for me will ya?"

"No sweat." he pig-fucked the cigarette and put it in the Marine's mouth. Drawing deeply on their cigarettes, they were closer than brothers even if they'd never seen each other before.

"Where ya goin'?"

"Home." he answered. It was answer enough.

The marine looked at him with undisguised envy, "Lucky bastard!"

"Maybe not so lucky. I'll be back in a month for another tour."

"Stupid fish," the marine laughed and then had a coughing-fit, "next they'll talk you into turning lifer," he gasped a choked chuckle.

"I got my reasons," he was on the defensive, "don't knock it unless you try it."

"No way Jose! To each his own. No way in hell that I'll extend for another six months. Man, I'm short...so short that lawyers shit on me and they're even lower than snakes. After I get out of the hospital I'll probably get my ticket home...back across the pond and home to The World."

"Well...tomorrow about this time I should be getting off the plane back home...scooping out all that round-eyed pussy." The thought of going home made him feel almost...happy.

"It's not the same as when we left you know," the Marine had suddenly turned serious; "you've been gone too long. Things are a changing. A friend of mine went back last month. They spat on him...called him every rotten name in the book. Said he killed babies and wasn't fit to walk the streets."

"You're crazy. Things like that don't happen back home," he angrily ground his cigarette into the dust, "we're fighting to keep them safe."

"O.K. Have it your way," the Marine held up his good arm as if to fend off the anger, "you'll find out soon enough for yourself. Sometimes I think that they're the only lucky ones," he indicated the row of dead marines in their body bags and then lapsed into a brooding silence and seemed to fall asleep.

A corpsman, who until then had been busy with more of the walking wounded, came over, and checked his bandage. "He's out of it," the corpsman said, "let him rest."

"What happened to the arm?"

"Booby trap. Crossbow bolt with shit smeared on the tip. Said he was two days in the boonies before they could bring him in."

"You guy's never heard of medevac[7]?"

The Corpsman bridled at the accusation, "Tell it to someone else, asshole. The medivac choppers tried to get them, the poor fuckers. The LZ was taking big stuff, incoming NVA 156mm Gook artillery...but they tried. Yeah, they tried then they died."

The little corpsman was being belligerent, and had the right to be. "Sorry, didn't mean anything by it. Just seems like a raw deal," he apologized.

"No offense taken, Marine...I see you been there a few times too."

"A few," he agreed, "but not like that."

To the east of the rising black smoke, he could make out a wing of phantoms systematically working the ridgeline over with napalm. Farther to the west, a mountaintop seemed to leap into the sky, and then disappear behind a huge dust cloud. Later they heard a sound like a small earthquake, and he knew that the B-52's were working the area over too. Soon "puff" would come, raining death on any surviving N.V.A. with its mini-cannons.

He glanced at the marine with the bandaged arm. The man's cigarette had burned down to his lips and the flesh was smoldering,

"Wake up Asshole, you're on fire!" He pulled the cigarette from the marines' mouth. There was no answer and then he realized that the man had died. "Corpsman!" he shouted.

The corpsman checked for signs of life, "He bought it," the corpsman's eyes moistened, "sometimes they go like that. It's the quiet

---

[7]   Medical evacuation helicopters were the lifeline of the Vietnam War. Affectionately known as medevacs or dust offs–a nickname originally taken from the radio call sign of Army chopper pilot Major Charles L. Kelly, who was killed in action on July 1, 1964–these Bell UH-1 Huey airborne ambulances and their brave crews saved the lives of thousands of wounded soldiers.

ones who don't cry or bitch much that are afixin' to die. God knows what was in the shit they smeared on the arrow. Come on, let's drag him over there with the others...they can bag him and tag him later."

He helped the "doc" drag the dead marine to his silent place in a line of bagged and tagged brothers. While helping carry the still warm body he had to keep reminding himself that he was going home. Hanging on to that reality by the thinnest of threads he told himself over and over, 'Don't lose it. You're goin' home...home...home...home.'

A few more marines wandered over and sat down. Doc returned to tending the walking wounded. Later, someone from Graves Registration arrived to "tag and bag" the dead marine. The process seemed coldly indifferent. They collected his papers, personal effects, dog tags, placed him in a body bag, tagged the bag, and registered it. The marine in charge of the operation joked with his friend, and neither one of them seemed affected by what was happening.

"Any news on that bird?" he asked the radioman.

"Keep your shit together. Things are getting pretty hairy around here. If it keeps up, we'll be completely cut off again. Right now, the only sure way in or out of here is by chopper."

Death could come anytime to claim them and with this too familiar angel would descend the perpetual paranoia with which they lived every minute of every day. He got up, walked to the other side of the bunker, and pissed on the sandbags. In the valley, he saw a jeep plowing through the dust and making its way to the heli-pad. As it came closer, he could make out Smitty, the Battalion clerk, who drove up to the helipad where he stopped and waited a minute for the dust cloud that followed the jeep to clear.

Buttoning his fly, he walked to meet him, "Smitty, you goin' home too?"

Smitty looked at him for a long moment before answering, "Nope, and looks like maybe neither are you. Hop-in, they want you back at battalion."

"Fuck you, like hell I am! Tell them that I left before you found me. Ain't no way in hell that I'm goin' back to the CP!" he had expected a sniper's bullet, maybe, but not being called back at the last minute.

"Wait-one, Brad, no-can-do. I didn't say they canceled your leave...they just want to see you before you go home."

Grudgingly he swung his kit bag into the jeep, "Alright, but I hope they make it short. There's a bird coming in any minute."

They rode in silence back to the battalion command post. He was furious: fucking green machine...why him? They pulled up in front of the C.P. The Chaplain was waiting, "Leave the kit bag in the jeep, and come sit over here with me for a minute, Brad."

"What's this all about Chaplin?"

"I'm Chaplain McDermit. Have a cigarette."

"Thanks," he took the cigarette, "now sir, what's this all about. I mean, I'm on my way home. If it's about the letter I got from home, I've already spoken to the other Chaplain about it...and I'm going back to take care of things."

"Letter?" Chaplain McDermit asked, and so he briefly filled him in.

"Better sit down, son. I'm afraid I have some hard news for you. Your mother was killed four days ago."

"What?" he whispered. Suddenly he couldn't speak. His throat constricted into a dry lump as he sat there... and he could hear an ocean roaring in his ears...his mind spun, and he heard the distant rumble of the chariot of the sun, or was it just the rolling thunder of an artillery barrage, and ...his mother was...dead...her? At home?

"How...? Why...?" He started to shake.

"They don't know. It took the Red Cross four days to find you out here. Are you religious?" The Chaplain asked.

"Sir...I'm just a marine." his hands wouldn't stop shaking. "There must have been something...an accident...an illness...something."

"She'd been shot and that's all we know," the Chaplain's voice seemed to echo. "That's all we know," he repeated, "and that your mother was shot to death four days ago. Try to understand, Son."

"Understand what? God's will?" he said bitterly, "I spend my time here in this goddamned shit-hole, and someone shoots my mother at home...God's will! When I was here protecting America who was protecting her?"

The tears were forming in his eyes, slowly blurring his vision until he willed them away. In spite of the heat, he was very cold...and couldn't speak. A corpsman handed him some water and a pill, which he swallowed automatically. The Chaplain pressed a pack of cigarettes into his hand, "Take these. Here are some more pills. When you get to Da Nang a friend of mine will be waiting for you, and he'll get you a priority flight to Japan, and from there, God willing, back home. Remember...God is with you." He took the cigarettes and the pills. He would never forget this simple gesture of human kindness.

"The pills will help you, but if you take too many of them, you'll sleep...so lay off them if you can."

His mind began to blur...he got back in the jeep with Smitty. "Sorry Brad," Smitty said.

He didn't have strength to do more than nod back at Smitty. He only wanted to get home as soon as possible and...and then what? He didn't know. Four days already dead. Had she been murdered? Would he have to kill the person responsible? The pills numbed him. He neither felt nor knew anything as he was passed from helicopter to helicopter, like the marines in their body bags, until he finally reached Da Nang. Once there a young chaplain took him in tow and bullied him on to a C-123 Cargo Plane heading to Iwakuni Airbase in Japan where he arrived still in his jungle fatigues. Although they had taken his rifle from him in Da Nang, they had neglected to check his pockets. He still had a grenade that he took out of his pocket, shrugged, and stuffed it back. It would remain with him throughout the entire flight home.

Iwakuni was like a dream, which passed in a blur, but with no time to freshen up...yet another Chaplain...and then, without even enough time to breathe the clean air of Japan, another flight out to Seattle Washington. The flight was populated by returning veterans, all of them Army, and all in their dress uniforms...pretty stewardesses serving beer and Jack Daniels, while there he sat, totally spaced out from the pills; a lone marine, dusty, smelling of the jungle, with a look on his face that discouraged conversation.

Somewhere between Japan and Seattle, he slept but didn't dream; he slipped into an oily dark sea, and it was cold. And then he felt someone going for his throat! He reached out and grabbed the frightened stewardess that had tried to wake him. One of his hands was tightening painfully on the side of her face. It would leave a bruise. He released her with a muttered apology. She had mumbled something about marines being animals. He felt bad and he wanted to say more to her, but when they disembarked at the airport, she avoided him completely.

The other flight attendants gave him cold looks as he walked into the terminal... he was alone, had no money, still dressed in jungle fatigues, and in great need of a bath. He looked around in vain for the promised chaplain who was supposed to meet him, but as his fellow passengers thinned out, meeting loved ones, enjoying their first reunion in a year, he was left sitting on a plastic chair watching people who stared curiously at him, but no one come forward to tell him what to do next.

'The Marine Corps,' he thought, 'SNAFU: situation normal, all fucked up.' They had sent him off and had forgotten to tell anyone he was coming. He was tired and slipping his hand in his pocket, felt the grenade and thought, 'don't they know that there's a war on, and at this minute people that they might even know are killing and being killed?'

People continued to walk by...some stared and then politely looked away. Then, seemingly out of nowhere, someone came over and stood over him. "You're a bit out of uniform, Marine." It was an Army Sergeant Major in full dress uniform.

"Just got in from the 'Nam. I'm on emergency leave. Got to get back to Wisconsin for my mothers' funeral."

"Look," the Sergeant said, "I'm supposed to be working liaison for returning dogfaces. No one mentioned anything about a grunt-marine. I'm off duty now, so let's go to my place, I'll fix you something to eat, you can shower, and I'll check with the Marines and try to get you sorted out. Maybe they can find out who you belong to."

He nodded in agreement, got up, and let the Sergeant shepherd him through the airport. He didn't have anything to lose, and besides...nothing mattered. They got into an Army staff car and as they drove through the streets of Seattle, he watched the people from the passenger seat and noticed that a lot had changed—the hemlines had gone almost all the way up to the ass-hole.

"Been gone a long time?" the Sergeant said without taking his eyes off the road.

"Eleven plus months," he answered.

The Sergeant gave a low whistle, "Long time all right. Then you're in for some surprises...like that," he indicated four mini-skirted girls that strolled by as they stopped for a red light. The girls turned and smiled at him; or were they just impressed by the car?

"The dresses are a lot shorter now," his host observed, "too bad we can't make any time in uniform now, with the anti-war protesters making it a crime for anyone to be in the service."

"Fuck 'em all," he said. The important thing now was to just get back and settle things.

After a while, they pulled up to a ranch styled house in a suburban area...'nice lawn', he thought, 'even got a stone fox in the yard.'

"Well, here we are...home...at least it's my parent's house. Have you ever been to Seattle? No? Well, it's probably the best place on earth. Nice people...plenty of jobs, and the sky's the limit." Getting out of the car, he allowed the Sergeant usher him into the rambling ranch-style Seattle home.

"The bathroom's the first door on the right; down that small hall, there...you'll find soap, towels, and everything you need. There's some shaving kit in the medicine cabinet. Use it. Throw your clothes outside; they have a washer and dryer here, so you can get them back in about an hour. In the meantime, I'll make some calls and put something in the oven to heat."

He would do it by the numbers: shit, shower, shave, eat, and get the hell on his way back home. Throwing his clothes into the hall as directed they both heard the metallic sound of the grenade hitting the tiled floor. The Sergeant, startled, picked it up, and said, "I best dispose of this before you get arrested." Not knowing what to say, he said nothing, so only nodded.

In the shower he opened the hot water and let it clean most of the clinging stink and dust as he looked down at his body through the billowing steam clouds and thought, 'God, I've lost weight!' He hadn't had time to look at himself in Vietnam. Too busy. His body was...skinny.

Brown from the sun, no not brown but more of a sickly yellow. He got out of the shower and looked in the mirror. What looked back at him was something, and someone, he had never known. At least his mother wouldn't have to see him.

As he started to shave there came a knock at the door. "Throw out the under pants too."

The Sergeant's ignorance was amusing. "Don't wear any underpants in the 'Nam," he said.

An uneasy silence was followed by, "I'll set you out some of mine and a shirt and pair of jeans. They might be a bit big on you but they can't let you go around in your utilities, and that lack of underpants...is creepy."

That was fine by him. It didn't matter...nothing mattered. He popped another pill. They weren't half-bad and definitely took the edge off everything. He wrapped himself in the robe the sergeant had thoughtfully placed by the door. There were even bedroom slippers together with the promised clothes and underpants, and a small tote bag for his things. He would keep his jungle boots, though; they were like a second pair of feet. What impressed him most was the flush toilet; he didn't have to use it, but he flushed it a few times anyway just to watch the water go down. He had missed flush toilets as much as having something cold to drink.

After dressing, he followed his nose to the kitchen and sat down to a meal of bacon and eggs, a big gallon glass bottle of milk, which he drank greedily, followed by cup after cup of black coffee, as his host stared incredulously. He hadn't tasted cold milk since he shipped out for the 'Nam. The sergeant watched him eat in silence, forking more food on his plate, and refilling his glass when he'd emptied it. When he finally could eat no more, the sergeant went over to the refrigerator, brought back two cans of ice-cold Olympia beer, and said, "I got through to the Marine contingent down at the port. They say to bring you on down. They'll have some tickets for you...Chicago, and then Madison Wisconsin. You got any money?"

"Nothing." he said, "except for what was in my pockets."

"The grenade isn't going to be much use here. I'll take it back to the base tomorrow. Doesn't anybody check anything anymore?" he was half-amused, "I mean, walking around Seattle international airport and God knows how many other airports, with a grenade in your pocket!"

"Well, no one asked me for it," he said defensively, "and it felt good sitting there in my pocket. I don't suppose I could keep it."

"Not a chance. As it is, I'm going to have to cook up a story about how I 'found' it in the wastepaper basket back in the terminal after our Army boys passed through."

Listen," he said, changing the subject, "they said that they'd give you a few hundred dollars advance on your back pay down at the base, but if they don't, I'm going to give you a hundred up front, and you can send it back when you get home."

The offer was genuine, and he felt like there were still a few good people back home worth fighting for after all. "Thanks but let's wait until we see what the "crotch" will cough up. But thanks anyway."

They left the house and drove down to the Naval Station. A sergeant from the M.P.'s escorted them to the disbursing section where a clerk handed him an envelope with tickets, and counted out two hundred dollars in tens and twenties with a curt, "Sign here, it'll be deducted from your pay." Mechanically, he signed.

The Army Sergeant turned to the clerk. "Don't you people have a uniform issue here? He's on emergency leave and doesn't have a proper uniform."

"This is a navy base and the Marine contingent doesn't have a store of spare uniforms. I'm sorry, he'll have to go back the way he is."

They left the base and returned to the airport. He was cleaner, well fed, and hoped that someday he could repay this strange man, but knew that he couldn't, and also that it didn't matter. They shook hands and said goodbye. After the sergeant left, he realized that he never even asked the man his name. He boarded the plane for Chicago and promptly fell into another deep sleep and he dreamed, or did he? Was he ever awake?

• • •

The mosquitoes were bothering him. He looked through the steady falling rain, straining in an attempt to make out movement, but there was nothing...all was quiet, except for the frogs and the never ceasing drizzle of the monsoon. He knew that the frogs were a great alarm system—if they were quiet then watch out! From time to time, someone shot up a sickly yellow flair and the rice paddy was transformed into a grotesque vision of Dante's Inferno...shadows twisting with a life of their own, followed by total silence as even the frogs seemed to hold their breath...everything frozen in time, and finally, darkness covered the land like a black burial shroud.

With the passing of that small sickly miniature sun struggling to shed some light through the ever-present monsoon clouds, life returned to normal; the chorus of frogs singing in the rain keeping him company as he sat in his foxhole, deep in freezing cold water. They were two marines in every hole, with fifty percent alert, one slept if he could while the other kept watch. He heard movement...someone was sneaking through the rice paddy. He could smell them, the smell of fish heads and unwashed bodies. He twisted the safety pin out of a hand grenade and released the spoon. As the spoon flew, he waited two more seconds before throwing the grenade in the general direction of the noise. There was an explosion and suddenly the entire area erupted in tracer rounds...red and green, incoming green from the AK47's and outgoing red. He heard the whine of incoming mortar rounds, and from down the line came the cry, "incoming...incoming! Fix Bayonets!"

• • •

"Incoming!"

He jumped forward in his seat...then, realizing that he had dozed again; he sank back into the cushions. People looked up at him in alarm, but another soldier sitting across the aisle just smiled and gave him thumbs up. Over the speaker, he could hear the professionally warm voice of the stewardess, "We are on their final approach to O'Hare field. Please fasten your seat belts and observe the no smoking sign. We hope you have had a pleasant flight with us."

He would have a two-hour layover in O'Hare, a short flight to Truex Airport in Madison, and then twenty minutes down US Highway 51 to home. He considered calling his stepfather to let him know that he was coming but gave it up as a bad choice; he had never met the man and couldn't help the gut feeling that the man was, if not guilty, at least responsible. So, instead, he decided to call his Aunt Eldorae who lived in Chicago.

He dialed the number, waited a few rings, and then a man answered...his Uncle Johnny, "John, this is Tim. I'm at O'Hare." He almost used "Brad" but back here in The World people knew him by "Tim" and he silently told himself he would have to get used to it.

There was a long moment of silence. "Thank God the Red Cross found you. Have you called Grandma or Donald and let them know you're coming? When's your flight out?"

"I've got a flight in two hours. It should get me to Madison at about seven tonight. I haven't called anyone yet."

"We'll call them for you then, and someone'll meet you at the airport. One second, Eldorae wants to talk to you."

His aunt took the phone, "Tim? Are you all right?" he could feel the tension in her voice, and asked himself, was he? Was he all right?

"I guess so," he answered, "do you know how it happened?" he waited through a long silence, which made him wonder if they had been disconnected, until finally she answered, "I'm coming to you. I'll see you at the terminal restaurant in about a half an hour."

She handed the phone back to his Uncle. He could hear her talking to John as he muffled the phone, but it was clear by the background conversation they were having that she would be coming alone. John un-muffled the phone and asked him if he needed money.

"No, but thank you." They would all be coming up for the funeral and he'd see John then. He had never been especially close to Uncle John, a soft-spoken taciturn man who seemed to hold everyone at arm's length. Uncle Johnny had lost half his face in Guadalcanal, and only now, it occurred to him that this stoicism might have been the result of years of rehab and reconstruction. They did a great job on his face except that he would never be able force his muscles into a smile again. John was also a

Roman Catholic and therefore not well liked by the rest of the family. Eldorae had converted to Catholicism for Johnny; a move that the stoic Norwegian Methodists in the family had taken years to forgive. His other Uncle, Wally, had served with John, and fate, always fickle, saw to it that he never got a scratch during the entire war. Both of his uncles had been proud when he followed family tradition and had enlisted in the Corps.

He grabbed a table in the restaurant, ordered a bacon lettuce and tomato sandwich and coffee, and then hunkered down to wait for his aunt. While eating he observed the other customers talking happily, making plans, and seemingly totally oblivious to the death and destruction going on 10,000 miles away. That old saying from WWII kept passing through his mind, 'Don't they know there's a war on?'

Finally, five cigarettes and three cups of coffee later, she arrived. His aunt carried her tall thin frame with dignity but her eyes betrayed the depth of her grief. At first, he thought she might try to hug him, but the moment passed, and instead, she just sat down and grasped his hand. He saw that she had been crying and her hands shook as she held her cigarette.

"You asked me how it happened. I couldn't tell you on the phone, but it's safe here," she paused and looked into his eyes, then continued, "Burke killed her."

"What? Who?" he didn't understand.

"Leo, your so-called step-father, got drunk, forgot who he was—where he was, and killed her. Toward the end, he would get drunk and go back to W.W.II. Leo was a fifty missioner with a chest full of medals and an officer in the old Army Air Force. He stayed in too...twenty-year man. Oh, they'll try to cover it up, him and his rich bitch of a sister. But, we'll get them both. She killed my sister." She never once removed her eyes from his, not even when the tears started softly rolling down her cheeks.

"But how do you know?" he asked. His aunt was a strange woman. He remembered a visit they had a month before he shipped out to boot camp. They'd been sitting on the porch listing to the crickets. His mother was in the kitchen making coffee. His aunt had leaned close to him and, in a confidential whisper, informed him that everything was going to be fine. He would survive the war. He asked her why she was so certain. She smiled...and said the crickets told her. He realized she was serious and possibly a little insane. Thinking back, he remembered another time when she said the crickets told her that John Kennedy would be killed...and four months later the President was dead. This time there was no talk of crickets, "Surely she must have written to you?"

"Yes," he admitted, "There were problems. She mentioned that he was drinking heavily again...had lost his job, and she sounded depressed. I never met him; Leo came into her life after I left for Vietnam. Someone from her past, she told me." he didn't tell Eldorae about the last letter she wrote describing a reoccurring dream that haunted her; she was in a room and in the middle of that room was a coffin. She walked to the coffin, looked in, and saw herself, then she heard a knock on the door and she knew it was Leo...his stepfather. She knew that if she opened the door then what she saw in the coffin would come true. In her dream, she opened the door, and she wrote that now she was afraid of what might come next.

His aunt's voice brought him back to the present, "We called her every week. At first, she seemed happy enough with the new marriage. I never liked him much myself, even when they first met twenty-five years ago when Leo and Charlie, your father, were fighting it out for Lenore. Charlie won and Leo never forgave them. After the first month or so, your mother started getting depressed. She sounded dead inside...until about a week ago when she got your letter saying that you were coming home on leave. She was busy making up your room, buying special foods...calling up your friends, and generally acting like the old Lenore we all loved. And then...we got a call from Grandma telling us that she was dead," she paused a moment and then whispered, "she was pregnant. Did she tell you?"

'Pregnant?' he thought, 'A lost brother or sister?' and then he forced himself to answer, "She never told me." He felt a crushing double loss, one for the mother whose life ended with that terrifying gunshot, and for the unborn, that never had a chance to live. He wanted to continue talking, but he was numb...and he felt that something had been left undone, as if he had walked out the door and forgotten to turn off the lights. They both were chain smoking and the ashtray began to fill as she told him stories of their life together during the big depression. He knew them from listening to his mother and grandmother, but didn't have the heart to interrupt her as she re-lived memories of how they had all slept in one bed, and how they had left the farm to get an education in town at their Aunt Dora's house. She talked about their World War II generation, "the greatest generation", which had made The World a better place to live in.

'So, this was the better world they created.' he thought. His mother was dead and, with her, a brother or sister he might have known and this fact left him empty inside. He felt himself slipping in and out of reality, and stopped paying attention to what his aunt was saying. He was sitting listening to his Aunt talking to him, but he couldn't make out the words, and then, he would be back in Vietnam, or remembering glimpses of being with his mother in a thousand different places, all of which sprang painfully into his mind, only to slip away and evaporate like an early morning fog.

"They're calling for boarding," she said.

"What?"

"They're calling your flight, Tim. Better get going."

"You're right, I better get going. I'll see you at the funeral."

"Stay, Tim," she said, "we can all drive up tomorrow. You can stay in our Jimmy's room. He's away at college...you've been through enough. Come home with me and let us take care of you." She was pleading. But he couldn't go home with her. He didn't have the strength to help her and he knew that he couldn't help himself either. There was something important he had to do. He had to get home and so, he apologized, thanked her for the offer, and explained that he had to go home and see for himself. They touched hands again, and he felt his mother in her touch, then she walked him to the embarkation gate where she hugged him goodbye for the last time.

The plane was a puddle-jumper. A small jet used for the short hops between Chicago and all points North, West, East, or South. The first thing he noticed was that the stewardess was over thirty. Evidently, the younger girls got the West or East Coast runs and the over the hill set were relegated to the nowhere flights. She came over to him and started up a conversation.

"You're a Marine aren't you." she smiled.

"Yes I am." he returned her smile.

"I can always tell," she said. "Just back from Vietnam?"

"Yes. I'm going home on leave," she was an attractive woman, "how did you know I'm a marine?"

"I was married to a marine," she smiled. "I shouldn't be doing this, but do you mind if I sit down next to you?"

"Be my guest," he wondered for a moment if this old woman of 30 was trying to pick him up. She sat down and straightened the folds of her tight mini-skirt. He looked at her...thirty or not she was still built like a brick shit house, "Where's he stationed?"

"Who?" she asked.

"Your husband. You said he was a marine."

He waited to see how this would play out.

"He always wanted to be a career marine...a lifer," she looked past him, out through the porthole, "and he was killed five years ago in Vietnam. He was one of the first advisors to go in. So, when he was killed, I came home to Chicago and got my old job back with the airline. I fought hard for it...it's not every day that a woman my age can pick up where she left off."

"I'm sorry about your husband," he said. Her husband had been killed five years ago back when he had been a sophomore in high school, "it seems like the war's been going on forever."

"I hate the war," she said vehemently, "I hate everything about it. Guys like you...returning veterans...you've got to get them to stop it." He didn't know what to say and realized she was expecting something. Perversely his first instinct was to lash out at her, and that gut feeling made him feel ashamed. Stop the war? Stop what they were fighting for? Make everything they sacrificed for worthless? What did she want him to say?

"Look," he said, "I'm sorry about your old man. He was a marine, died a hero, and knew what he was doing. I'm a marine too. While I was over in Vietnam, my mother was killed...shot to death, and I'm going home to bury her. When the funeral is over, I am going back to Vietnam to kill some more Cong for our country. This is our duty and what we signed up for."

She looked at him; her eyes softened, and seemed to lose some of their intensity. She wasn't angry...only sad as she said, "God help you, Marine. Things are changing and you had better change with them. The war's wrong. Nobody's on your side any more. When you feel like talking give me a call."

She wrote her number on a piece of paper and handed it to him, "This is where I'm staying when in town. I share an apartment with a couple of friends. It's not far from the airport. Give me a call when you get your head together." She got up and walked into the forward compartment. He took the address and considered throwing it away. Then he folded it and put it into his breast pocket. Mentally he upgraded here age to twenty-eight or so and wondered if she had any kids. Maybe he'd call her. But wishes were one thing and reality another, or as his grandmother had always said, 'wish in one hand, shit in the other, and see which you get more of'.

He didn't get a chance to talk to her again during the short flight. It seemed that they had just finished climbing when they were already descending and circling Madison. As he looked down at the city bathed in the neon glow of early evening, he remembered his short career as a student in the University. Rising slightly in his seat, he thought he could make out the campus not far from the brilliantly illuminated State capital building. He was coming home.

When they landed and started taxing to the terminal he had the feeling that something was out of place; something wasn't right. This was the terminal...but not the terminal he had left a year before. What he saw was modern...slick and clean. He hesitated at the ramp. A stewardess was wishing the passengers farewell.

"Excuse me...but is this Madison?" he asked, feeling foolish.

"Of course, sir, unless somebody's misplaced it." She smiled at him, but she wasn't amused.

"When last I was here things seemed different," he said as he started down the boarding ramp.

"Things are different," she answered, "this is the new field. You must have left from old Truax field. We don't use it anymore."

"I guess that explains everything...things are different." he said, and wished he hadn't brought the subject up.

Home on leave before shipping out to Vietnam he had said goodbye to his mother at home, and then, his Uncle had driven both he and Linda, the niece of the man who would marry his mother some months later, to the airport. Linda...he never stopped thinking about her. She had practically moved in with them and he entertained a hope that they would end up like the people in the books and movies. He would go off to war, and she would be waiting when he came home, walking down the ramp...his mother and Linda together...but it was Linda who would count the most...because they would be getting married...but it realities soon make dreams vanish. After shipping out for Vietnam, she never answered his letters. It was as if Linda was only a dream. Three months later, he heard she was married. His mother had written shortly after her own marriage to give him the news. He never heard from her again and burned her picture in a futile attempt to purge himself of her memory. Everything always goes full circle, and the past, mixed with the present, would be a distant shadow, but at the same time, always a dark silhouette mocking life.

He walked past a dozing security man. The other passengers had already taken their bags from the conveyor belt and left...he waited...considered taking a cab, and then saw Donald walking in through the automatic door. Don hadn't changed...still tall and dressed in a leather flight jacket, easily standing a full head above everyone else in the lobby. He remembered trying to keep up with Donald when they'd go hunting...him taking two steps to every one of his Uncles' mile long strides.

Donald noticed him and walked over...he thrust out his hand. "Sorry your homecoming couldn't have been a better one. The cars outside. Got any bags?" he asked while extending his strong hand, which was calloused from work.

"No, just what I'm carrying."

They stood silently looking at one another for a minute. Neither knew what to say to the other, and then finally Donald shrugged, cleared his throat, and said, "Well, best get going then. Ma's waiting up for you back at her apartment. You can stay with me at my place if you'd rather..."

"Naw. But thanks anyway. Grandma's place'll be fine."

They walked out of brightly lit terminal and climbed into the old Nash Rambler that had seen better days, and drove in silence down new streets...and out of Madison. He didn't recognize anything until they hit highway 51. Traffic was lite...and he remembered that it had been that way since the completion of the new interstate, I-90 some years before. Highway 51 was already starting to die like everything else. They passed closed diners and darkened filling stations. Everything seemed covered with age and death. He should have died in Vietnam. It would have been better that way. He should have died...not her.

His Uncle broke the silence, "Do you want we should kill that bastard Leo?"

His Uncle had just offered to help him plan and execute a murder, "Maybe." he answered, "but it isn't clear what happened...at least not to me, and these things take time...and planning. Revenge, they say, is a dish best served cold."

"No one told you!" his uncle shot him an incredulous glance, "I would have thought that someone must have said something about how she died."

"I talked with Eldorae...but you know what that's like...what do you think happened?"

"I don't know, Tim. They say she killed herself...but either way, that bastard's responsible."

"How do they say she did it?" he was starting to feel sick.

"They said she used a doubled barreled shotgun...your Fox...the one she bought you for your seventeenth birthday."

"Jesus Fucking Christ!" he couldn't believe it.

"They say she shot herself twice. Once in the chest and again in the stomach." Donald was harassed and he could see that his Uncle was also still in shock. Don was a hard man, but tonight was the first time he saw him close to tears. "They said she just pressed the barrels...against her...and reached down with them long arms of hers and..." Don couldn't go on.

"Both barrels?" he asked.

"Yes...both barrels..."

He tried to picture it...he started shaking again... "Donald?"

"What?"

"There's just one thing wrong; the Fox[8] had only one trigger. In order to fire both barrels you would have to pull the trigger twice...no one could do that...no way, just no way she could have shot herself with a twelve-gage shotgun, pick the damn thing up, and then shoot again."

---

[8] Savage-Fox Single Trigger SxS 12 Gauge Shotgun. 30" vent rib barrels with dual sight beads, 2 3/4" chambers, single non-selective trigger, choked improved modified and full, blued barrels.

CHAPTER 2

The road flowed like a great black river, snaking its way passed farmhouses, whose yard lights were ringed with halos, shining yellow-blue through the chilled October ground-fog. In the East, a huge yellow-red Harvest Moon was rising; reminding him of Halloween and crisp green snow apples.

His mother loved harkening to the call of adventure, and would drive endlessly on nights like this; heading to nowhere in particular, simply following the small graveled country roads, and enjoying the cool October air as it flowed through the partially opened windows filling the night with the promise of approaching winter.

He glanced at his Uncle remembering how October had also been the opening of the hunting season that heralded the beginning of their endless treks into the wilderness in search of solitude and that special companionship that only men could share as they satiated their primordial hunting instincts. He would go with his Uncle and, in the company of men, comb the woods and marshes for game that was already more and more scarce in a world rapidly destroying and polluting what had once been a cornucopia of wild game a mere generation or two before. How quickly things change, he reflected, and now he never wanted to see another gun, or rough it by a campfire...he only wanted to sleep...and make up his mind if he should kill again—this time to take a life for purely personal reasons; following the code of vengeance, honor, and obligation. Those once meaningful words paled in light of his months of warfare and he thought, 'for what?'

In Vietnam, he had learned that there was nothing easier than taking a human life...and after a while killing became the norm for them. They would go on patrol, search, and destroy anything that lived and then return to whatever hill or village they were holding for the

41

night. If they were lucky enough to make it through the night's terrors, they would saddle-up and move out once again, to take more lives until the shadows reclaimed the day, when they would return to the questionable safety of the perimeter to spend yet another night in hell...and so the endless cycle repeated itself day by day...night by terrifying night.

'Yes', he thought, 'nothing would be easier than finding Leo and waste the bastard', but he sensed that it wouldn't be enough to make the ache go away.

Did his mother leave a note, something that could lead him to the answers he so desperately needed? Why had she let Leo kill her...or why had she allowed him to drive her to suicide? 'She must have left something behind, a note or an unsent letter,' he thought.

"She must have left a note, or something," he said.

Donald glanced over from his driving, "No. Nothing. I saw her after work on Friday. We talked about you coming home. She seemed happy. I knew things hadn't been going well between her and Leo. She must have written to you about it." Again, the statement was almost an unsaid accusation: She must have written, so why hadn't anyone done something about it in time to save her?

"Her letters were confused." he didn't feel like going into it.

"Well," Donald continued, "she seemed to be coming out of it when she learned that you would be home in a few days," he paused and then almost whispered his voice husky, "I should have done something...should have seen it coming, but you know how she was...sort of shut every one out of her world, except for Leo. She got so that she didn't speak to anyone but him. I always felt she was hiding something, or maybe protecting him."

Donald slowed down for a curve. "She wrote me that he'd been drinking. I didn't know that he'd been an alcoholic until she told me about it in one of her last letters," he explained to his Uncle. Her letters from home seemed to take on more significance now that she was gone.

Most lifers were hard drinkers, borderline alcoholics, and Leo was no exception. Twenty years in the air force had made that habit into an addiction and the bottle was probably the reason he had only risen to the rank of Major. In the end, there was no cure. Once an alcoholic always an alcoholic...he knew that eventually, they all crawl back into the bottle. He had known two distinct types of hard drinkers...the quiet type who settled into a happy stupor, and a more dangers vicious brooder...capable of violent outbursts that would have been unthinkable when sober. Leo was the latter of the two.

His mother had written him that when sober Leo retained no memory of his violent side and seemed grief-stricken and contrite when she had told him what he had done. He wondered if he had the right to take the life of this man that his mother tried to reach...and for better or worse, had loved.

In the Marines, he had learned that the best answer is to kill. When in doubt...kill   the enemy. But the enemy was in Vietnam, and he was back in The World, sitting beside his uncle, going home to bury his mother. He had not come home to kill...and then he realized that they all wanted him to kill Leo. They expected it of him...as if he had become the instrument of their vengeance. Whatever happened he would put off any decision until he had sat down and talked to Leo, face to face.

"She was a proud woman, Donald. She wouldn't take help from anyone."

He remembered her as she was on the night before he shipped out...she had seemed so small and fragile. She finally seemed to realize she was alone...he would leave her and possibly never return. It was then she broke down and for the first time in his life, he had seen her cry. He held her and tried to comfort her...but she wouldn't be comforted, just shuddered, and sobbed uncontrollably. When his ride to the airport arrived and he had gone away leaving her alone, Leo had entered her life and offered to fill that vacuum. Guilt and anger conflicted for ascendance as he realized that by leaving home he had helped to killed his own mother, and that while he hadn't been the instrument of her death, he had certainly opened the door, which let it slip into her world.

"O.K., I won't judge him for now."

Donald seemed relieved, "It's been a rough couple of days on all of us," he said.

The city limits sign proclaimed *Welcome to Dunkirk Population*

5555. 'The four fives must have been someone's idea of a joke,' he thought. Dunkirk was the town where he had grown up; where he had lived for eighteen years under the unforgiving microscope that is found only in small close-knit communities. Living in a small town, you were a part of the general entertainment, examined...or more correctly vivisected...by every member of the community. You knew your place, and more importantly, everyone else did as well; and God help you if you stepped out of it, even for an instant. Driving through the small community, every street, and house filled him with memories. He blotted out the swarming images of a thousand other times...pushing them back. It was difficult enough dealing with the present.

Donald parked the car outside of his grandmother Haziel's apartment building. She had moved into the building shortly after he enlisted. Haziel was an independent Old Norse woman, used to living alone and taking care of herself; a touchstone reminder of the depression years where she had lost a son and supported her three infant daughters after her husband died from blood poisoning. She married again to a character out of the wild west of the 1880's, a man who had known many of the legends who were being commercialized by the western sagas seen weekly on every television set in America. Donald's father, simply known as Barber, had been married before to a Jewish woman.

She died leaving Barber to provide for grown sons and daughters, some of whom migrated to Dunkirk when he married Haziel. Donald was the surviving son, his older brother having died of lockjaw on the hardscrabble farm that they were living in at the time. He remembered his mother talking about her baby brother, and thought he heard her voice whispering in his ear again as memories of long ago started to surface, *"We girls were living on a farm down in Hainerville. Freddy was playing in the yard, and stepped on a nail. A few days later, he was so sick...I sat with him, and then Freddy was gone. I cried and cried, and then looked across the field and saw a little blue bird flying away, and I knew that he was happy...somewhere."*

They had another son after that and called him Donald, who became his best friend and the closest thing he had to an older brother. They both loved this tough old woman, and although she never expressed any emotion, he knew she loved the both of them with a fierce love.

Following Donald up the weary old staircase that smelled of age and neglect he remembered that his mother had always called the place a miserable firetrap, but Haziel had refused to move in with her and Leo. She worried about his grandmother being caught in a tenement fire and burning to death in her sleep. Looking about saw there were no fire escapes...one-way in and out...it was a tinderbox...another death trap for the old, the poor, and the infirm. At least it was clean without the ever-present stench of urine he had encountered in so many tenements since leaving home.

Across the street was the old Mandt Wagon Works, which had been the pride of the community for a hundred years and was reborn as the Highway Trailer right after World War I; now growing feeble, and beginning to deteriorate like most of the businesses in any small Wisconsin town no longer being buoyed up by war contracts.

They didn't knock...just opened the door and walked into her kitchen. She had three rooms that were furnished in second hand furniture. Her walls were papered haphazardly, in disparate bits and pieces, which she had hung herself. A pot of alarmingly strong black Norwegian coffee bubbled thickly on the gas range. Haziel was a Norwegian's Norwegian; Old Country, speaking a Norse that had been extinct for eighty years, and she was an American because of an accident of birth. She spoke Norwegian before she learned English in the public school. He knew that she grieved, and also that she would never show that grief.

Welcoming him as if he had only been gone a day or two, Haziel grumbled and fussed, making them sit at her small kitchen table and drink coffee while she prepared a quick meal of salt pork and eggs. No mention was made of his mother or the funeral and yet her eyes betrayed her grief and anger.

Sitting there, home at last, he felt everything catching up with him, as if he had reached the end of his endurance, and the miles of travel, doubt, and the uncertainty that had always been a few steps behind, tapped him on the shoulder making him feel weak...his head was burning and he felt all the hours and miles of his odyssey solidify into a solid weight pressing down on his soul. His throat constricted and it became difficult to breathe...yet at the same time he wanted another cigarette and absently touched the half-empty pack of Camels in his coat pocket, and then took his hand away as if he had touched a burning coal; he didn't dare smoke in her house. Smoking was one of the many things the formidable old woman wouldn't tolerate. It amused him to think that he, a Marine, a professional killer, could be so intimidated by one frail old woman. Donald finished his coffee, excused himself, and went home. They were alone now.

She walked over to the cupboard and took something out, "Your Ma drew this," she said handing him a charcoal sketch his mother had done of him before he left for Vietnam. "I remember when she drew it. You were just back from that Marine boot-camp."

Reverently holding it in his hands, he studied the drawing and noticed once again how every line and shading had been carefully worked into a beautiful rendition of a young man who, like her, had died—but yet still lived and was now holding her drawing. It was delicately done and he could feel the love she had for him then, but couldn't help wondering if she would still have loved the man he had become as much as she loved the boy he was in the picture.

"She drew this before Leo," she said. He could feel the bitter hate in that simple statement, and more, he knew that she had starting counting time from before and after Leo came into his mother's life, 'like B.L. and A.L.' he thought, sardonically comparing it with AD and BC.

He had spent so little of his last leave with her. Linda had taken up most of his time. Of course, he had never dreamed that of the two of them, his mother would be the one to die...it had never been part of his way of thinking then. Even his last night home had been spent with Linda. His mother certainly felt excluded and no longer a part of his life. He knew that she felt he had deserted her, first for the Marines and then for a girl she didn't like and most certainly didn't approve of. On the morning of his departure, she had made breakfast for the three of them. The meal had been tense. He had wanted her to take Linda in, share her home with Linda until he returned, but she had pronounced the idea unthinkable. He had been angered by her obstinacy. To him it had seemed like the perfect solution. He would go off to war and the two people he cared for most would look after one another until he returned. But then, he hadn't figured on Leo...or on Linda. He had left and now she was dead. 'Why her?' he had fought for his country...was willing to kill and even die for America, but why had America allowed someone to take the life of his mother? The inevitable thought surfaced: 'Why had they let her die when he was ten thousand miles away fighting for them?'

. . .

In the Marines there is a saying... 'the pay-back's a mother fuck.' Was this the payback for killing other mother's sons or for killing someone's mother who was crouched in that explicitly Asian way, in her black pajamas, with that great conical mama-san hat hiding her face, cradling her head in her hands and crying out in terror as the high explosives tore her village to pieces; finally splattering her against the torn landscape...because someone suspected the village was a V.C. stronghold and he had done his job exceptionally well...first round right on target...and the barrage that followed left nothing to chance. Nothing came out of that village alive. And then just to make sure, he led a team down to the village...descending into hell with no hope of resurrection on the third day or on any other; performing that all-important body count, and placing a bullet in the head of anything still moving, man or beast.

. . .

His grandmother's voice brought him back from that long dead Vietnamese village; pulling him back from that damn village, and from the body count, where, in his mind, the dead woman was now his own mother, dressed in torn black pajamas...with a battered hat covering part of her face while the flies swarmed and he knew he had to get out of his grandmother's house before he started losing it again.

47

A DESTINY OF MEMORIES

"I have to see the house where she died." he said.

Her eyes met his, faded blue looking into the darker winter-frosted eyes of this grandson she had always loved and cared for, and he felt her pain as she said, "It's so late. You need sleep. Stay here...it isn't much but I have a cot in the back room."

Looking around the dingy apartment, he knew that this would be home to him for a while. "Thank you Grandma. I'll be back," he promise, "I just have to see it...the house where she...died."

She nodded her head in resignation, "Bullhead," she muttered, "do what you have to...but at least put a jacket on. It's cold out there."

He gave a short laugh, "Don't worry...I didn't come home to catch cold and die." Then he thought, 'No. I should have died over there. Now it's too late.'

Walking to the house where she died he was as wary as he ever had been when on patrol in Vietnam—creeping through the deserted late-night streets of this small mid-western town, knowing that now he was a stranger here, and yet this town had been a part of him once. He was a ghost, returned from Vietnam to a place that he had waited a long time to see and touch, but now that he was finally back—he relived memories of a past that was now dead. Yet he had survived; and being alive was a good thing. He lit another cigarette, letting the match momentarily warm his hands and then continued walking toward the bridge that spanned a river that was called the Yahara River, which in the native Ho-Chunk Winnebago tribe dialogue is "maa'ii yahara," or the 'shown' river. What would the river show him this time?

The street was once constructed of red bricks, piece by piece, artfully joined in such a way as to not leave as much as a seam between the bricks that formed it; a long curved crescent joining the railroad tracks on the East Side with the bridge and the river marking the beginning of the more prosperous homes in the West Side. It had since been blacktopped and became a part of Highway 51, first made famous by Bob Dylan in his 1962 song "Highway 51" that continued its journey through the center of the town; bring a prosperity, which had lasted until the super highway I-90 made such things a memory.

48

As he walked, he remembered how the town had been filled with life as it had bustled in that yesterday's hot summer's sun.

. . .

The street and sidewalks shimmered in the hot summer sun...burning the soles of his bare feet causing him to dance like an Indian Fakir over hot coals. The old men, veterans of what was once called "the Great War," sat in the shade of the store awning saying, "Hot today...hot enough to fry an egg on the sidewalk."

. . .

He wondered if they ever tried it—actually frying that proverbial egg, and if so, how it might have tasted.' The old red brick road was there, buried deep under the asphalt of progress. It lived beneath the surface of death—its time-weakened heart still beating softly and whispering of things that were and could be once again. Then that momentary subtle warmth of memory, which had filtered through the black gum of the asphalt road, evaporated as all memories must, leaving him with the reality of this bitter cold night of discontent.

He stopped walking and warily glanced around as the combat instinct took over again and told him that something had changed. It was a stoplight that had been added to the crossing at the end of the block, right next to the Jew's shop. Nothing dangerous, he told himself, as the adrenalin wore off leaving him feeling both annoyed and uneasy. The stoplight didn't understand about the street or the shop where the town Jew had sold them fig bars and Red Goose Shoes long before. The Jew's shop belonged to the time of the red brick road—a time before his friend Keith Fuller burned to death in the Highway Trailer, depriving Vietnam of yet another sacrificial victim. He glared at the light but it just blinked back at him with its amber eye, and in the silent corners of his mind, he asked over and over again why she had to die.

He continued walking and without remembering how he got there, found himself on the bridge, leaning against its painted metal railing, staring down into the inky waters, which neither hid nor revealed a thing. He wondered why people jumped and what it would take to make a decision to join the river, and why she had decided to die when he was so close to coming home. He could have stopped what happened if he hadn't been away fighting other people's battles while at home she was left alone to lose the biggest battle of her life. A fever was burning inside of him. He had to find an answer. She was gone now and would never know how close he had come to being able to save her. If he had arrived six days earlier, everything would have been different, but time had run out for both of them. He would search the house for a note or an explanation.

'It too late to make a difference', he thought, as his hands folded around the cold rail of the bridge. Any answer could help take away some of the pain. He tried to cry then—hands pressing hard into the cold metal—but nothing came. There were no tears to fill the emptiness inside as distance, time, and death were already blurring his memories of her...the pictures, which came to his mind, were strangely conflicting. Some were of a strong-willed protective woman, providing for her family and giving everything she had to those she loved, and another, of an aging frail woman of 46, clinging to him, a hurt broken bird saying good-by for the last time to summer, and no longer able to wait for next year's spring.

She had cultivated a simple faith and optimism that was an almost naive belief in the power of life and love. Had she killed herself or was there more? Either way she had been killed by circumstances that were both of her own making and also beyond her control. In the end, did it matter? Did anything really matter? Dead was dead. His mind reached out to touch the stars shining distantly from the cold night sky. 'Does it matter,' he asked them, 'that she used the 12 gage double-barreled shotgun she gave me for my seventeenth birthday? Does it matter that she had pressed the barrels to her heart and pulled the trigger once...and then once again? Does it matter that she hadn't aimed for the face? Was it because of a woman's vanity that she chose her chest?' 'No', he answered those unfeeling stars, 'a woman wouldn't choose to die that way, and certainly not a woman who had been deathly afraid of guns all her life, and was terrified of their noise. She wouldn't shoot her own baby growing inside.' Their only answer was eternal cold silence.

CHAPTER 3

He continued walking and remembering. The memories would always be a part of him, and try as he might, he would never be able to shake them. No amount of running would allow him to outdistance the phantoms that pursued, and when he finally stopped running, the rapacious sights and sounds of his past would catch up, strangling all of his tomorrows, just as they were already strangling his todays. Memories long-past merged and morphed into memories of other nights, and with those more recent memories came the gut-wrenching fear of having to control his every movement, even his breathing—being watchful not to make that one single last mistake which would cost his life and possibly the lives of those depending on him. He was walking "point"; the first man in—eyes and ears of the prowling killing machine that was a Marine night recon patrol—a thinking and breathing machine which was a predator made up of many individual living parts—going on only so long as the point man didn't make any mistakes and when a mistake was made, the machine would die, and its parts would be gone, forever dead and forgotten, doomed to pull the chariot of the sun for eternity.

• • •

He stared into the dark Indochinese night—black and soulless as only the monsoon can make it. There were no stars, and no moon, just the eternal darkness and the steady drip of the rain. He prayed silently to every god worth the name to grant him another day of living. God, Jesus, Buddha, or Satan, it didn't matter. He prayed the simple silent pray of wanting to live saying this mantra over and over again 'please let me live'. Their listening post (LP) consisted of a three man team, far forward of the perimeter, a circular nest made in the tall grass, which had been hastily set up for the night; their duty to listen for the enemy and report on how many were coming and what arms they carried—and most important of all; to survive. They sat, back to back; forming a rough triangle, with the PRC-10 radio equipped with headsets next to them its dull olive green invisible in the black night. They would answer by using pre-arranged clicks caused by briefly pressing on the handset send switch. Two clicks, for all quiet. Three clicks for an enemy approaching and then, in a whisper, a brief situation report (SitRep).

"Delta one to firefly 7, sitrep," the CP checked in with them.

'Click Click" the microphone answered giving the code for 'No joy tonight and we are still alive.'

The night, moonless and with no stars visible, continued endlessly. They didn't dare to move or make any noise, and no one fell asleep, until finally came the welcome sweet soft dawn light, which seeped diffidently through the endless overcast.

And then there were other times, when he was still new to Asia—a time of dust, sun and fear and he remembered that he looked up and saw her for the first time. She crouched patiently squatting for hours, flat-footed on the ground, and yet still having a certain birdlike grace. Her ageless wrinkled face was that of a "watcher", a silent watcher—one who waits—Asia incarnate waiting apathetically for what must assuredly happen.

The trucks filled with Marines drove past her; an endless dust filled caravan of replacements, faces, both white and black, so young...soon to become ageless, but still new enough to willingly approach the gates of death and pain.

She watched them, silently hating every truck filled with these alien invaders of her land. After the last truck had past, and the dust had settled, she gracefully walked back into her small candle shop, picked one of the candles off the shelf, and admired her handy-work.

When the explosions came, she carefully put the candle back as she hummed something learned from her mother before the French left for the last time—a tune which helped to drown out the sounds of men screaming in agony. When the sound of the wounded and dying finally became too much for her, she smiled and closed the door.

A DESTINY OF MEMORIES

• • •

He snapped back to the dark cold October night as his mind screamed, 'why and for what'. Had everything been for this? He looked around at the uncaring vacant streets with the cold soulless stars still laughing down from the night sky. Was this the America that his friends had died for—the America that had allowed his mother's life to be snuffed out while he was fighting ten thousand miles from home? 'Going back to The World,' they had said. Was this that world—the place that had lived in their memory and was the only thing that kept them going during the long months of terror and agony, which had shattered their youthful illusions? Was this new reality worth fighting for? If not, then what was missing?

Everything was missing—nothing was as before. The new reality of war and the faces of the dead who haunted his waking hours, and became a permanent fixture of his dreams, had tainted everything. He wanted to be somewhere else...to be somebody else and not the boy who left this quiet mid-western village and returned a man cold and dead inside, yet still alive enough that his warm breath formed a fog of doubt as it mixed with the cold Wisconsin air.

Walking those near-deserted streets, he forced himself to think of the summer things—like rainy Sunday mornings when he read the papers together with his mother, spreading them on the living room floor as he lost himself in the lands of Alley Oop and Lil Abner. Or when he picked the first dandy-lion of the season and gave it to her. Then there was the way that the sun would always break through the storm clouds making everything right and warm again. But that reality was gone now, beyond his reach, and he was living a today in which he was chained to a chariot pulled by the twin horses of death and loss.

Her death was the reality now—not that bounding terrifying animal that charged screaming, clawing, and ripping men to shreds that he had become so familiar with; deaths which would always live on in the minds of anyone who had ever been in the 'Nam—but a new kind of death, one which was killing his soul as it had killed her body there in her own home, on a quiet side street, the squeeze of a trigger followed by a bang that her ears never heard; her trembling body losing all conscious thought—her individuality fading into black nothingness with no golden chariot of the sun to pull—no, that chariot was reserved for warriors, not victims.

He had seen men shake in cold fear knowing that their death was coming, and then there were others who died silently, slipping into death, barely creating a ripple on the surface of reality—gasping for a last breath and then giving up as their eyes clouded over, forever sealing their final thoughts from the living. He wondered if it been that way for her. His mind drifted, feet mechanically moving, only halting when he arrived at the house where she died.

All the lights were blazing; the curtains pulled back allowing the golden light to flood the porch and fight the darkness that clung stubbornly to the bushes. He stood for a moment, looking at the house and remembering a letter she wrote telling him that she and Leo had purchased the home that she had lived in as a teenage girl. The old clapboard house held many good memories for her and she wrote her books and poems there, nursing a hope that when he returned they would become a family. Yet now, less than a year after her marriage, she was gone, and that family was shattered and dead like the brother or sister she was carrying inside of her.

The house was located across from the local cemetery, the silent street like the river Styx separating the realm of the living from the dead. He crossed that river and felt like a modern day Odysseus tricking Charon into poling his boat between the two worlds. Climbing up the porch steps, he almost knocked on the front door, hesitated, and asked himself if he should knock. Undecided, he moved with jungle-learned stealth to the window and carefully looked in. A man was sitting in the easy chair, empty beer, and whiskey bottles on the floor, and he was apparently asleep or passed out. He recognized him from the pictures she had sent; this was Leo, his stepfather. Returning to the front door, he opened it, and still moving silently, took a seat across from him. He had snapped the necks of men once called his enemy, and it would be no problem to let this broken down shell of a man sleep for eternity. 'A simple thing.' he thought, and he could leave as unobserved as he had entered. The next person to open the door would just find a drunk that had fallen out of his chair and snapped his neck in this bad luck house owned by a bad luck family. Yet somehow it didn't seem enough...a quick death would be too easy for this man. Instead, he tore a page out of the local paper, wadded it up, and threw it with some force into the man's face. He didn't trust himself to walk over and shake the drunk awake.

Leo woke with a start; held his head in his hands, and rubbed his jaw, the stubble making a faint scratching sound. Then he focused his bloodshot eyes in recognition and said, "Tim, you made it. We delayed the funeral until this Friday to give them time to find you."

Leo rose unsteadily his feet and reached out to offer his hand, and then let it fall when it became apparent that he would make no move to take it. Leo then sank heavily back into the easy chair, the weight of his body making it squeal slightly as it slid a few inches back. He seemed to be waiting for him to say something.

"How did she die?" he finally asked. "Did she leave a note? Where were you when it happened?" Each question hit Leo like a physical blow. He winced as the questions hit home.

Leo reached down, picked up a mostly near empty bottle, chugged the dregs and said, "I told the police I don't remember anything. I'd been drinking and was sleeping it off, dead to the world. I guess the shots woke me, and I must have come downstairs and found her...must have called my sister before I passed out again because when I woke up she'd driven down from Madison, called the police, and took charge of everything," he rambled on, "you probably remember her—Linda's mom."

"I remember Linda," he said, locking eyes with Leo trying to see any sign of loss looking back out at him, but Leo's steel grey eyes showed nothing at all, no sign of emotion, so he asked, "Did you kill her?"

Expecting a denial, or anger, he was surprised when Leo answered evenly, "I don't know...don't remember anything, but I pray to God that I had nothing to do with this. My sister said that she told the police she believed it was suicide. I suppose that if it was I am just as responsible as if I had killed her myself." Leo paused then continued, "If you're looking for the man really responsible, it was your father, Charles Sweeney. He destroyed her. If you want, we can take the car, drive down to Janesville, and kill him."

Leo fell silent, and then rubbed his eyes and said, "Excuse me, have to wash my face," then pulled himself out of the chair, staggered unsteadily to the kitchen where he noisily splashed water on his face, and cleared his nostrils. When he returned, Leo seemed a bit more sober. "They didn't find a note," he offered.

"Mind if I look around?"

"Help yourself. She died in the downstairs bedroom over there," Leo indicated a closed door off the living room. "I'm going upstairs and lay down. Pam, my daughter, will be home soon and if you need anything just ask her." Once again, Leo seemed to hesitate, not knowing what to do, his eyes searching for something. Then, giving it up, he turned and climbed the stairs to the second floor, disappearing into the dark hallway.

He stared at the closed bedroom door and then got up, twisted the doorknob, and pushed. The hinges made a slight squeal of protest as the door swung open. He noted that the room had been scrubbed clean and smelled of bleach and Lysol, which almost choked him. There were no bloodstains in the room and the bed was made as if for an expected guest. He sat next to the bed on a straight-backed chair and started going through the drawers in the antique roller top desk which held his portable electric Smith Corona typewriter, reams of paper, assorted bills, and documents—and a finished manuscript. She had evidently been using the room as an office and a quiet place to collect her thoughts and put things down on paper. She called her book "Althea" and had worked on it for years. The story was based on a girl living in biblical Israel. Looking closely, he noted that the cover page appeared to be splattered with dried blood. If there would be a note surely it would be here, he thought.

As he dug through his mother's things, he heard the unmistakable engine of a VW bug as it pulled into the driveway. He recognized that sound, it was his VW...the one he had almost lived in during his last month in the states, commuting nightly from Dunkirk to Madison while he was dating Linda. The car door slammed, and he heard the click of heals as someone walked across the porch and opened the front door. It could only be Pam, and as she walked into the living room, he recognized her from the picture his mother had sent him. The door to the bedroom was open so she walked in. "Tim?" she said. She seemed confused and he knew she wanted to hug him, but he made no move so she just stood there, letting her hands fall limply to her side. Pam was a picturesque, tall girl, with sculptured features, and seeing her in person, he agreed with his mother's assessment that she would make a good model. She started to sit on the bed, then, something crossed her face, and so instead, she pulled up a stool and sat next to him at the writing desk.

Reaching out she gently touched his arm, "I'm glad they found you in time. It was hard for them to find you."

"They found me," he said as he flinched from her touch. He noticed the momentary hurt that crossed her face as she hastily withdrew her hand.

"I can't tell you how sorry we are," she said, "I only moved here a month ago, but I loved her like a second mother."

"But she wasn't, was she." he said. She seemed confused, "She wasn't your mother, was she? Your mother is still alive." he knew he was being unkind but he didn't care.

He saw tears forming in her eyes, "No." she said. "And you're right, she wasn't my mother."

"So what happened," he asked.

She took a deep breath and seemed to pull herself together, and answered in a toneless voice, "we don't know. I was with Linda at my aunt's house. We got a call from Dad and my Aunt rushed to the car and left. She didn't tell us anything until the next day. Apparently your mother..." she choked up, and couldn't finish.

"I know," he said. "She apparently took her own life and the life of the baby inside of her."

Pam seemed shocked by this and mumbled, "She was ..."

"Yes," he said, "she was."

"I had no idea." She started crying.

"She didn't leave a note," he said. "Nothing to indicate suicide?"

She wiped her eyes, "I know that she was so happy and excited with you coming home and all. We had no indication that anything like this could happen. The police are still looking into it."

He didn't want to push harder. This 17-year-old girl was at her breaking point and he didn't want to hurt her further. "Help me look around," he said, "and let's go through her things."

She nodded assent, they started going through his mother's papers, and as they sifted through the remnants of his mother's life, she talked about Linda. "Linda let me read your letters," she offered.

"Letters she never answered," he said.

"They were beautiful letters but Linda was already seeing someone else soon after you left. She got pregnant, married, and now he is a soldier serving in Vietnam. She...they... didn't know how to tell you."

"Yeah, well life sucks." he answered. He remembered burning Linda's picture and letting the ashes fall into the sea as he stood on the deck of the troop ship on its way to Vietnam, burying her at sea together with the fiction of what might have been.

They continued searching his mother's files. So much was missing, including many of his letters he had sent home to her from Vietnam. "Nothing." he said in disgust.

"My aunt cleaned up after they took her away. She wanted things to be clean for your homecoming. We have a different room for you if don't want to stay here...this is where she died. You can have mine ... I'll be staying with Linda anyway."

"All I want are the keys to my Bug." he knew that would leave her without transportation, but really didn't give a damn.

After a slight hesitation, she handed him the keys, "Of course," she said, "I can use Dad's car. After the funeral, he's checking himself into the VA hospital for rehab." Then she added, "I wish you would at least consider staying here. This is your home too."

He thought it over and then answered, "No. This is where she died. I don't have a home anymore but I do have a place to stay. Where did they take her? Which funeral home?"

"Skaalen's Funeral Home, over on the east side," she answered.

He knew the place well. When he was thirteen, he had delivered newspapers to that mausoleum of the dead, and to the strange bald bachelor owner who lived above it. "I'll see you around," he said.

She looked like she wanted to say more, but all he saw in her eyes was a combination of both pity and fear. She nodded gave him the keys and watched him as he walked out the door and got in his VW bug that still smelled of her perfume.

He drove past the cemetery, and he could feel her there; his mother, sitting in the back seat...her eyes drilling into the back of his neck. He knew that a quick glance into the rear view mirror would reveal nothing but an empty street, but he was afraid to look for fear that she wouldn't be there after all. Let her ride with him, he thought. By the time he reached his grandmother's tumble down apartment building, his mother was gone and as she departed, loneliness and guilt filled the vacuum she left behind. He should never have left home he mused as he pulled to the curb, locked the car, and walked up to his grandmother's small apartment.

As usual, the door wasn't locked. It protested on rusty hinges as he opened it and he was afraid that he might have awaken her, but she was waiting up for him, and without exchanging many words, she led him to the small alcove in which a cot had been set up. The curtained alcove offered some privacy. The bathroom and shower, she reminded, was communal and located down the hall. He didn't bother to undress, just stretched out on the cot, and closed his eyes, listing to the steady tick-tock of the wall clock from the other room.

He prayed then, asking God why he had ever been born, and as the enormity of his loss finally sunk in, for the first time he silently cried, for her...for himself...and for everything. He cried like a motherless child as the wings of sleep enfolded him and he sank into the darkness of his dreams.

CHAPTER 4

He was in a shell-hole, his body felt shattered like pieces of broken glass, the world around him was a desolate void and he called out for help but no one answered. He was buried with just his head, shoulder, and one arm protruding from the debris.

He called out "God help me." But there was no answer. "Jesus! Satan! Anyone! Are you there?" he cried, but again there was no answer until finally something came to the top of the shell hole and looked down at him. As he reached out his arm came into focus...it was covered in blood, but he felt no pain. "Help me. Please help me!"

It smiled down at him and said, "Do you accept my help without reservation?"

He knew that this was Death and yet he said, "Yes!" Then Death or perhaps it was Satan, or maybe only just the corpsman, looked at him with its empty eyes, and answered, "Take my hand and I'll put your world back together."

He reached out, took the hand that was offered, and was pulled out of the shell hole, then he woke up on a stretcher drenched in someone else's blood.

• • •

The sound of his grandmother moving about in her tiny kitchen making coffee and eggs woke him from the dream, which had haunted him since the day Biff had called artillery fire on their positions. The curtain allowed him some small amount of privacy, but after Vietnam, it was a luxury. 'A new day and another dawn', he thought. He glanced at the wall clock and realized he had slept most of the day away. The strong black coffee from yesterday was still simmering like black molten lava on the stove. She poured him a cup, which changed from the color of black tar to a more appetizing chocolate when the milk was added and she also brought him a greasy platter of butter- burned eggs. As he ate, he realized just how hungry he must be to wolf it down without complaint.

"This is how I remember your mother," she said, holding an ancient picture of his mother at around age eighteen.

"She was a fine looking woman," he said softly.

"Of course she had her faults, lord knows we all have, but most of the time she was good and kind."

Yes, he thought, she was good and kind and yet there were many times when she annoyed him. 'She lived a good life filled with bad lies', he mused, 'yet only the good lives on, and everything else disappears into the fog of time.'

"They say she looks so natural," she said, "but of course I haven't gone to see her yet, but those that did say she looks real nice."

"I'm sure they did a good job on her." he didn't bother to hide the sarcasm in his voice. She seemed to overlook it, or was so distracted by the death of her oldest child that she didn't notice.

"They're awfully good these days, you know."

He changed the subject, "The funeral's set for this week?"

"Yes. They didn't think you would make it in time. A body only keeps so long, you know. The Red Cross couldn't find you, but you're here now, and that's all that matters. Nothing keeps forever, Tim, the flesh is perishable, and only the soul lives on." She was as hard and cold as the Fjords from which her family had immigrated two generations before.

"It's getting late," he said, not wanting to think about it. "I must have slept most of the day away."

"I let you sleep," she poured him another cup of coffee, "and you were moaning something awful."

He nodded. "Just a bad dream, Grandma, it's ok now." Nevertheless, he knew it was more than that. "I want to drive up to the Funeral home and see her," he said. "Don't wait up for me."

"Door's never locked," she answered with a smile. He knew it was true and would always be so.

It was still light; the Wisconsin October afternoon was slowly giving way to the evening hours when the city would bustle for a while with people, and then, they would crawl into their beds and watch the late evening news on a portable black and white TV. But now, in this twilight hour, the city came to life; workmen on their way to the taverns before going home, farmers driving into to town to buy necessities, and high school kids, much like himself not so long before, hanging out at the local pool hall or bowling alley.

He drove the VW over the railroad tracks that bisected Main Street into Dunkirk Central and Dunkirk East Side, downshifted to second as the little VW engine labored manfully to climb the steep hill. The Funeral home looked much as it had when he delivered newspapers to its somewhat mysterious balding owner who lived upstairs. Painted a brilliant white, the building was now catching the last rays of the setting sun, its six neo-Grecian pillars casting shadows, which seemed to suck the light from the Art Nouveau stained glass windows. The lawn, although well kept, was feeling the early October frost, and had turned dead yellow in places. The owner/operator, Mr. Olsen, answered the door. Olsen was a professional caretaker of the dead and attempted to give consolation to the living. He had always pictured him, somehow, as an ancient Egyptian embalmer, whose long years of practice had oiled his professional voice and mannerism to a high level of perfection. Everything from Olsen's smile to his cold effeminate handshake, reminded him of an old Bella Lagousie movie. This small-town eternal bachelor shared a special intimacy with the many by-products of death, which would lay naked on his embalming table as he worked through the night to make them seem natural.

"Have you seen Mother yet?" Olson asked. He didn't answer and was amused by Olsen's reference to the husk as 'Mother' as if the man were in some way related to her.

"I just got back from Vietnam last night," he said.

Olsen blinked and then said, in his professionally soothing voice, "Yes, yes of course. It must be a shock—a horrible shock."

He didn't answer—couldn't answer, just nodded.

After a long and somewhat embarrassing silence Olsen cleared his throat, 'She's resting in the next room"

63

'Resting?' he thought, 'Do the dead rest here? Certainly not the grateful dead who waited for him to join them.' Unable to help himself he quoted Luke 8:52 to this strange whispering companion of death. "Resting? You mean that she has not died, but is only asleep?" he said as the bitterness welled out of some dark recess in what was left of his soul and seemed to build a tangible barrier between Olsen and himself.

Maintaining stoic professionalism, Olsen remained silent and ushered him into the viewing room. "I'll leave you with Mother." Olson said, giving his arm a gentle squeeze, which sent a chill up his spine.

Approaching the coffin, he knew that a part of him also lay lifeless in that box. The lid was open and a mirror reflected her face, but it was the face of a stranger. The image of his mother as he had last seen her contrasted with this dead wax figure in the rectangular box, its eyes closed, and its hands clasped over what he knew was the terrible wound inflicted by two 12-gage shotgun blasts; one to her heart and the second a bit closer to her womb. His vision blurred as the first waves of grief washed over him like a cold arctic wind. Approaching her casket, he wiped the collecting moisture from his eyes, and looked at the thing that had once been his mother. Olsen had dressed her in a red dress and in her folded hands; he saw a white lily...that symbol of rebirth, a flower that she had always loved. In spite of Olson's best work, her face was furrowed with deep lines...lines he didn't remember seeing before. Without the cosmetics, he knew her face would be even more wax-like, just like the dead he had seen in Vietnam. Where had she disappeared to when that delicate animating force some call the soul left this thing behind. Reaching out he touched her cheek, and left his hand resting against her cold dead face then he gave her a final caress, knowing that it was something he had to do in farewell. As he mouthed a wordless goodbye, he willed her to wake up and walk away with him; and as he looked down for the last time at the shell that had once been his mother, he remembered his first meeting with death. He was very young; maybe three or four, and they'd been walking along the summer-dusty road. They stopped for moment by the body of his pet dog, which had been hit by a car.

. . .

"Get up, Pepper," he said, "get up!" he reached down to help Pepper out of the dust, but the dog was cold and stiff. His mother gently pulled him away and said something about Pepper going to heaven and as they walked away from his dog, she comforted him with her arms. He looked back once and wondered why his dog wouldn't follow them.

. . .

This empty shell would never again be a part of his world, and as he remembered her playing the piano with her long tapered fingers, he wiped a tear from his eye; while far away and ghost-like her favorite music, "*Clair de Lune*" echoed in the corners of his mind. Once again, he didn't look back, and as he left, he felt her eyes staring at him behind closed lids while the tune played on, and on as he fled the house of the dead and drove back down that steep hill to the center of town, not knowing exactly where he intended to go, but just relieved to be moving again. Slowing at the crossing, he remembered the day that a car full of high school athletes didn't stop in time, skidded through the flashing barrier, and were crushed by a speeding freight train. All were killed and the local high school had mourned for a week until it was time to move on to things that are more important; like the junior prom.

Driving through the twilight of the city he saw ghosts of the past walking the streets...phantom visions of his boyhood. He drove past the post office, which had been decorated with murals that had been commissioned by the Treasury Department during the Great depression as part of the Public Works Art Project. The wall boasted a mural called "*Air Mail Service*" painted by Lewandowski back in 1940. Once there had been benches outside the building, filled with old men talking and smoking, but gone now. The benches had been removed along with the old men whom had either moved on, or died and been forgotten. Somehow this caused him to think about something he had studied so long ago; a saying attributed to Gertrud Stein, in which the WWI vets were called "a lost generation." His was another "lost generation," he mused, a generation who would return to home finding that everything was and always would be "business as usual."

Thinking about literature reminded him that he wanted to see his English teacher, Steve Fortney, the man who had made his senior year in Dunkirk High School bearable. He drove to Steve's home, and tapped lightly on the door, which Steve opened immediately. It was almost as if Steve had been expecting him. They shook hands, without saying anything, and he felt accepted for the first time since his return. Sitting down in the living room, Steve poured him a glass of his good homemade straw colored wine. "It's good wine, isn't it?" Steve asked.

Looking at the golden nectar in his wine glass, he held it to the light, and took another sip, made a decision and then answered, "Grapes and a bit of wheat?" he guessed.

Steve smiled, "I trained you well."

Some things will always live on, no matter what, he thought. More than anyone else Steve had encouraged him to write. He had repaid his mentor by trying to be the best writer he could with the limited experience he had. A volume of Tolstoy seemed to look down from the bookshelf, which took up an entire wall, and he thought the look was one of approval.

"I'm sorry about your mother." Steve paused, "I saw her only last Friday."

Not knowing what was expected of him, he had no answer other than a short, "Yeah, that's life."

Steve went on, "She seemed excited—told me how great it was going to be to see you again after all this time. And then, without warning..."

Without knowing why he confessed, "I extended my tour in Vietnam to come back and see her."

"I know. She told me that too. You don't have to go back." Steve sipped that golden summer wine. "I spoke with Wally, and he thinks he can get that extension in Vietnam cancelled. Wally also told me that Leo killed her." Steve gave him a searching look.

"Wally said that?" he queried. Wally was his mother's boss, and friend, and maybe even more than that. They had worked together for years in the Insurance agency where she was his agent and loyal secretary.

"During World War II Wally was in England with the Red Cross; said he still has contacts and can probably swing it. Tim, you don't have to go back."

"Wally said that about Leo?" he repeated the question.

Steve nodded. "It's a hard thing that happened. Don't make it worse by going back."

While there was no reason to go back to a war he no longer believed in, the thought of staying in this country that had betrayed him left a bitter taste in his mouth that even Steve's wine couldn't wash away. "It doesn't make much difference now...about going back or staying, or if Leo killed her or not. She's dead, and nothing can change that, and there is no way that doing anything to Leo will ever bring her back." he paused, took a breath, and started to let it out. "As far as the war is concerned; no one knows anymore why they're fighting. You once told me you're a Johnsonian Democrat...well I got the Presidential Unit Citation from Johnson, but all it means in the end that I did his job of killing very well! We got the Citation for killing NVA on the DMZ (Demilitarized Zone) who were barely in their teens."

'God', he thought. 'Then what am I? Twenty and not old enough to vote or to drink, but god...how old am I on the inside?' "Those kids," he went on, "are trained from maybe the age of five, or six and they send them against us when they are old enough to carry a weapon. They didn't run and didn't give up until we killed them all. Everyone dies for nothing over there." He stared at the wine in his glass and thought, 'they sent them, they—the eternal they, all- knowing, all-powerful, and all wise... fuck them all.'

"There's a little rat-hole on a hill called KheSahn and another not so far away called ConThien," he continued, "the brass called them victories, but all I knew is that their dead stank just like ours out there in that hot sun. It's not about being good soldiers, neither for us nor for them. We fight the VC and the NVA and we all die, and bleed by the thousands for what we both believe in. We do it for America. But if this is America," he nodded toward the window, "then we don't know this America and America doesn't know us any longer either. Those VC and

NVA live in little shitty huts, without electricity or plumbing, but still leave their homes in the north, with maybe a RPG (Rocket Propelled Grenade) strapped to their back, and walk for months through the forests and jungles, find one of our bases, fire the damn thing, and walk back to get another one.

I knew a Gook back in a small French fort called BK-17. He spoke English and used to cut our hair. Found him one morning hanging from the perimeter wire. I asked myself...and for what? The barber is dead— his friends died later that night, when the North Vietnamese marched the villagers in front of them for human shields. First, we mowed down the villagers, and then the NVA. The bodies were everywhere and in the morning we bulldozed a trench and threw them into that muddy pit.

Back here it's business as usual, kids worrying about getting into college for that 2-S deferment[9], or if they will get a date for the homecoming dance while in a different world thousands of miles away, we live with death and dream about coming home to something better only to find when we get here, that the dream is gone—lost for us. As Wolf said, "You can't go home again," and I didn't understand it then but now I do. Sorry, Steve, I know this sounds crazy doesn't it."

Steve poured him another glass, "No. It doesn't sound crazy at all."

He didn't know if it was the wine, or just being with one of the few people he still felt comfortable with, but he continued to let it out. He told Steve about the endless voyage on the troop-ship from San Diego harbor to Da Nang Vietnam. Almost as soon as the ship left the harbor and hit "Bluewater" men were sick and puking their guts out. They'd been forced to bunk on hammocks stacked five high with only a few inches separating them from each other, with the bottom man avoiding, as best he could, the spew of vomit fomo the upper hammocks.

While crossing the Pacific they ran into a Typhoon just before they hit the Philippine Islands. He had heard about typhoons, but until then, could never have grasped the enormity of nature at its most violent until it overtook their troopship. Most of the time they had to stay in the hammocks, the vomit sloshing from one side of the bulkheads to the other. Those who could get up made it to the dining area, where

---

9   2-S Student deferment during the Vietnam War Era (temporary delay)

magnetized trays held fast to the metal tables while the waves would tilt the ship 45 degrees or more, and the food spilled out to mix with the sludge on the floor. They stood watch on the upper deck once every 24 hours during the typhoon; waves crashed over the top of the ship, and had to cling tenuously to the metal ladders and railings of the deck.

Steve's voice brought him back from the South China Sea to the living room in Dunkirk, "My brother left for Vietnam last Sunday." Steve said, "I worry a lot about him. Do you remember my brother?"

"I think I met him once. Where are they sending him?"

"A place called Danang." Steve answered. "He got drafted and became a medic."

"In the Marines we call them corpsmen and those guys are the bravest people I have ever known," and then, noticing the worry in Steve's eyes he went on, "I wouldn't worry too much. Danang is pretty far south and with any luck, he'll be assigned to a hospital and not a line company. It's a lot safer down there than up in the I Corps DMZ area. They have cold drinks, USO shows, and even a big PX (Post Exchange)."

As he reassured Steve, he felt like a traitor. A medic was eventually assigned to a line unit, and life expectancy for a medic was among the lowest of any member of a combat team. Their courage and their loyalty to the men they saved made them a choice target of opportunity for the Vietcong and NVA troops. They were even more of a target than the officers or the radiomen. 'How many more brothers, fathers, husbands, and lovers would be called upon to pull the chariot of the sun?' he wondered and also if someday he would meet Steve's brother, pulling that chariot.

He changed the subject, "I remember the day you bought this old house, and how hard you worked to make the floors shine...great wooden floors hiding underneath the linoleum. And then the moving day!"

"Moving day." Steve laughed, "That profound day of bumble bees and daffodils."

"We found the foam rubber feely."

"And drank that German beer with Dirty Old Man Gene."

"I remember him, Steve"

"And after all those good times they're still sitting here. The sun still rises. The town is mostly in the same place as it has always been...here on the banks of the Yahara River." Steve said.

He was silent for a while and then said, "And I guess that in the end, I lost."

Steve looked up sharply, "What do you mean?"

"Well," he said, "Here we are talking about good times, yet, I am still in that Green Killing Machine and I guess they'll send me back soon to join the others. I don't mind, really. At least there you know what's real and what isn't."

"Was it worth it?" Steve asked. "Was it worth dropping out of college for Vietnam?"

He hesitated and then carefully chose his answer, "I thought the experience would give me more maturity as a writer. I never considered the price."

"Did you learn anything?" Steve was the teacher again and he was the student once more.

"Yes, I think maybe I did. The real story isn't over there in the forests and jungles of Vietnam. It's here, in the small towns of America where the nation is taking sides, but not for or against the Vietcong or the North Vietnamese Army—no, the sides are for or against us, the poor bastards fighting over there. Maybe, if I live long enough, I can write something, if only for myself," then, changing the subject he added, "what about you, Steve, are you still writing your book?"

"I've only got one chapter left to finish 'El Novel.'"

It was a comfortable feeling, sitting in this room with his friend and mentor, drinking wine, and talking about the things that used to mean so much. He almost caught that elusive fragrance of that phantom world filled with the hope and all the misplaced loyalties that had set him on this path of destruction. "In the end, I should have stayed in College." He said.

"So you regret leaving?"

"Yes, but I still had to know. I had to know what it was like. I just couldn't sit in school when all this was going on."

Steve smiled, "That's the main reason why I wasn't very disturbed when you quit. Oh, I was angry with you at first, but then I realized that you had to be a part of things, to see what was happening with your own eyes. I always believed, and still do, that you will be going back to school someday."

"It's already been an eternity." He thought back on the school days at the U. The panty raids, the life in the dorm as a "dorm-dork", the competition for girls with the "frat-rats", the beer parties, and the days of study and jamming with his friend, he on the harmonica and Randy Ruckti on the guitar. Some of the very first Vets were filtering into the University, back from Vietnam, silent, older, and filled with a sadness that kept them apart from the others. They were unapproachable except by the other vets. When he had asked one how it was over there, he just smiled and changed the subject. That was long, long ago, and now he understood only too well what that smile meant.

"I know it seems like a long time." Steve said, "But in three years you've gained maturity and insight that wouldn't have been possible in a small town, or even on the campus. You participated, for good or for evil, in an event, which will change history. Sure, you might not think that the small part you played in an ugly little war made any difference, but it did, if only because you were there, and I believe that someday you will write about it. All this will be in your favor when you go back to school and hit the books," he paused, "you *are* going back aren't you?

"The GI bill is something I intend to take advantage of, if only to make them pay for what I went through."

There was a long break in the conversation, and he realized there wasn't much more to say. "I better get going. The funeral's tomorrow."

"You know we're here for you." Steve said, and clasped his hand.

"I know. I won't ever forget it. I'll see you tomorrow." Steve walked him to the door.

He left the warm living room and walked back to his car. It was already getting cold, but as he drove he tried to remember warmer times, but failed, and then let the night close back in around him. He didn't want to go back to the small apartment, and so drove to the lake, using the twisting back roads. As he drove, he could feel her again, sitting in the back seat, watching him; her dead eyes focused into the back of his neck. Once again he refused to look in the rear view mirror, and then, as suddenly as it had come, the feeling was gone—she was gone and he was freed from her dead gaze. In its place, loneliness filled him again, and as his hands were shaking so hard, he couldn't hold the steering wheel, so he pulled over on a little rise overlooking the lake where the cold clear sky and the great October moon's reflection danced in the myriad ripples that seemed to form miniature waves as they lapped against the shoreline. He thought he heard piano music muted but still audible in the stillness of the early evening. He sat there, in the car, waiting for an answer. After a while, knowing that there were no answers, he put the VW in gear and drove away, pushing the VW until it was doing over 90, racing through the tunnel of gnarled trees that formed a protective roof over the road; the speed and the flash of the green canopy above filled him with a fleeting happiness and he laughed as he heard the tires squeal in protest on the hairpin curves.

It was at the final sharp bend in the road, fittingly called "Dead Man's Curve" that he lost control of the car, skidded, instinctively turned the wheel against the direction of the skid, and somehow avoided the trees as the car slalomed between them until finally coming to a halt in a field where the engine promptly died. His hands were still shaking as he opened the door and tumbled out. It was then that he saw her, in the ditch, only he wasn't in Wisconsin any longer, he was back in Vietnam.

• • •

Looking down at her he knew that she should have died minutes ago, but somehow kept clinging to life...mangled, no hope left for her; he walked over to her broken body, tears eroding little trails in the dust that caked his face. He had to cry for her, she couldn't...she just looked at him, her eyes begging him to end it. It was then that he knew what was about to occur should never be allowed to happen again. He pulled his 0.45 Colt from the holster and walked over to her. He wanted to say that he was sorry for every fucking one of them, but he didn't know the words in Vietnamese. She still had her AK-47 (Kalashnikov AK-47 assault Rifle) beside her, but didn't have the strength to lift it...she glanced at it once, and then back at him. Her lips moved, but he didn't understand, and as he pointed his pistol at her, she smiled. She closed her eyes to make it easier for him, and he squeezed the trigger, watching her head explode as the 0.45 cal. round burst it into a bloody red mist.

. . .

Running to the dead girl, he reached down to her, but the night, and the jungle faded, and what he held was only a piece of dead wood. There would be no forgiveness for him, so when the shaking subsided, he walked back to the VW and saw that no damage had been done and for some unknown reason, once again, he stayed alive and he cursed his fate as he drove back to town, and to the small cot waiting for him at his grandmothers. There were two of them now, in the back seat, looking at him—his mother and the VC girl soldier. Tomorrow, he reassured himself, he would bury his dead and start again. He entered the apartment and sank into his cot, kicked off his shoes and socks, and prayed for a dreamless sleep.

CHAPTER 5

He thought that it should have been raining that day they buried his mother. It wasn't though, and instead of rain and gloom, it had the taste of the morning after a storm; everything having that crisp surreal clean feel to it. He would have preferred to bury her in the morning, because mornings were her times...she had always been at her best when the sun filled the world with light and birdsong, and as the day wore on, the shadows would weigh down on her until the night reclaimed her for its own. Now he knew that shadows never disappear, they only wait for the morning when they grow again, lengthening or shortening under the sun, and then, when twilight ends, are swallowed up by endless night, until the morning gives re-birth and the phantoms of the night become only memory revisited. She was only a fading memory now, like mist...gone...wind-scattered and the new days ahead would never really be quite the same without her.

She had been one of the most beautiful things in his life and now all that remained was her dried husk, life gone elsewhere, leaving memories as her only memorial. *Memories—he remembered a soft quiet time...a rainy Sunday afternoon, and when the rain stopped, there was a hot humid hush in the lush green foliage that formed the boarders of 5th street, which marked the dividing point between his house and the railroad tracks. That side of the road was simply called 'the Bank', because it formed an embankment that flowed down into the valley below, which held the coal yards, Sheldrup's feed-mill, and the railroad tracks; parallel iron ribbons running all the way from Chicago to Minneapolis in the North. The trees, heavily saturated with the summer rain, hung like wilted flowers; he could feel their wetness as he brushed his way through the low hanging branches walking that forbidden trail which snaked down the cliff and into the valley. His mother had forbidden* him to go over the Bank, so it was an absolutely desirable place for a small boy of five who had to explore the limits of his freedom. It was a feeling day; a day in which things happened. Each breath of humid air felt different; filled with expectancy, and he owned the day, it was his. He was alone, but he knew that the loneliness would pass when he went home, where he would sit on the couch with her, eat popcorn, and watch Have Gun Will Travel.

All of his friends had already disappeared down that mysterious trail, and only he, still heeding his Mother's warning, hesitated. Would she somehow know if he crossed that forbidden line...Mother's always seemed to know these things, he told himself...or would he run back to her, breathless with excitement and happily blurt out the whole thing; about his conquest of fear and the joy of flying free into the unknown? He knew then, and he knew now, that for the rest of his life, the Bank would always be his first milestone on the way to manhood.

"It's time to go" his Aunt's voice broke his musing. "You'll be riding with us, right behind the hearse."

The funeral procession seemed to go on for miles as the cars, headlights lit, solemnly followed the hearse. The local police directed traffic, and allowed the procession to proceed without any hindrance. No one said anything, just stared ahead at the black Cadillac Miller-Meteor that was carrying his mother to her final destination. People stopped and looked as the procession moved down Main Street, some took their hats off; others seemed to wipe a tear, and then look down. She had been well known and, by many, well loved. Also, the circumstances of her passing had become the number one interest in this small sleepy town.

Most of the cars parked on the road outside of the cemetery, but a few managed to follow the hearse to where it stopped not far from the newly violated earth; a deep trench that would be his Mother's home for eternity. Six men removed the casket placed it on a latticework of boards that formed a temporary covering over the black hungry maw of the waiting grave. A preacher was saying something, but he couldn't hear or understand the words. He was there, but detached, not a part of what was going on, just an observer standing next to the open grave, surrounded by people who couldn't meet his eyes. There is always an uncomfortable distance between the bereaved and the well-wishers, the curious, and sensation seekers. In Vietnam, he forced himself to become detached from everything around him that could make him uncomfortable, yet remained alert for any sense of danger. This skill allowed him to stay clinically aware of the most minute gesture, facial expression, or whisper from the people waiting impatiently for the funeral to be over. He was a ghost watching himself stand at the edge of infinity as they lowered the casket and then the people filed to the still open maw that would soon swallow her, stepping to the graveside and nervously throwing a handful of earth on the coffin lid. It seemed to him that with each enactment of that traditional gesture, the finality of her death was sealed.

He remained standing by the grave, acknowledging condolences with a nod...a handshake...feeling absolutely nothing except the pain of his guilt and loss. The grave now swallowed the polished wooden box with a decomposing husk inside; her physical remains while her soul, if there is such a thing, was being tossed like a ship at sea traveling in a void from which there would be no return.

The burial team looked at him, questioningly, and he nodded to them in assent. As they began filling the grave the sound the dirt, impacting on the coffin lid reverberated through him like a base drum. He felt nauseous as he glanced at the crowd, which was just now beginning to thin. All these people, he thought, paying their respects...had they actually loved her that much. Was it love, or curiosity? He could almost feel their thoughts; was it murder, suicide or an accident?

Leo's family were huddled together like frightened sheep encircled by predators. In the town's eyes, they were the ones responsible...the outsiders that didn't belong here. He saw Leo being led away by his sister, and after a moment, Linda paused, and then walked back to him; Linda—who had promised to wait for him, now ballooning in her last trimester and married to another soldier, who was serving in Vietnam. The pity in her eyes made him uncomfortable because he felt none for her, and the promise in her eyes disgusted him, so without a word, he turned his back. She gasped or choked, he didn't care which, and walked back to rejoin her family; he hoped that she was leaving his life forever.

Coming home was not a new beginning, but an ending. Constantly loyal—always faithful, he stood by the grave until finally he was alone with the cemetery attendants who waited impatiently to finish the job and return home to have lunch with their families. He nodded for them to finish covering her grave and waited until the last spade-full of dirt was tapped into a firm rectangular mound. They nodded to him, shouldered their spades, and left him to the silence of the dead.

Dropping to his knees, he pressed his hand into the fresh cold earth in a silent farewell. He wouldn't feel her eyes on him any longer; they were covered by a coffin lid and the traditional six feet of dirt. Now nothing remained except memories. As he crossed the cemetery, he did his best to avoid walking on the carefully tended graves. His friends and he had made midnight trips to the cemetery in search of night crawlers, under the theory that the dead provided worm food. He remembered how they had tried not to desecrate the graves in Vietnam, only taking cover from incoming in those strange family tombs, surrounded by a low wall, when absolutely necessary.

. . .

The convoy had stopped next to a Vietnamese cemetery located just outside of Hue. A funeral was taking place and, curious, he asked an English speaking ARVN what was going on.

"The family members are sending him into the next life," he was told.

"The next life?" he asked.

The ARVN (A soldier in the Army of the Republic of Vietnam) smiled, "Yes, but not today. These ceremonies can go on for years," he paused and then continued, "and we will be placing food gifts into his mouth, since he will soon be a respected ancestor. Lots of feasting, songs, and monks." And then, with a certain sadness he added, "Death is not a final ending of life but only a step into the next stage. Still the family is sad, since it is last time the soul will be here, next to its loved ones." It had been the first time he understood the Vietnamese reverence for the dead; a reverence, which somehow conflicted with their apparent disregard for life—the dead were only in transition; they would live again. The Vietnamese had souls!

. . .

Would she live again? He looked back at the new grave, then turning his back, began the walk down the hill and onto Riverside Road, which followed the winding Yahara River from the cemetery to the old milldam that had produced electricity for the small town and surrounding rural area since the turn of the century. He stopped for a moment and looked at the sill waters of the millpond, its mirror like surface reflecting the trees and the factories on the other bank and as the late afternoon sun moved silently into the West, he watched the shadows from the surrounding hills lengthen until the reflections were swallowed in the invading darkness, which spread over the water like deadly angels of death.

He continued walking up 4th street until the corner of fourth and Main where he paused at the office where she had worked for so manyyears with Wally Netterblad. The crisp black letters of the sign proclaimed, Netterblad Insurance Agency: 'We write it Right.' While standing there he debated whether to turn right on East Main, walk back toward the city hall, and visit the last home he had shared with her, or just chill and smoke a cigarette. Choosing the cigarette he lit one and held it between his thumb and forefinger, as he would a joint. He wanted a joint now, and took a long drag on the cigarette, letting it settle in his lungs before he exhaled. He remembered the first time he had turned on to weed. It was in Phu Bai during the monsoon...a base camp consisting of mud, tents, and holes in the ground and where when they couldn't sleep, and were half frozen from the cold wet, they had turned on together. There were four of them, Mac from San Francisco, two from Los Angeles, and he...the naive small-town kid from Wisconsin. They were all equally cold, wet, and afraid.

· · ·

Mac rolled the first joint, "They have good shit over here in the 'Nam." He lit the joint, took a deep hit, and passed it around.

When it was his turn, he hesitated and looked at Mac for direction. "Just like a cigarette, Brad," Mac said, "take it in deep, and hold it for as long as you can."

The grass burned his lungs and after a long moment, he exhaled.

"Take another," someone said. They encouraged him to continue until the roach burned his fingertips.

He felt happy and enjoyed this strange calm feeling that radiated from somewhere within and allowed him to ignore the dark wet reality of four scared boys huddling in a hole with a makeshift roof of ponchos holding back the rain.

· · ·

Back on Main Street, he took another drag on the cigarette, closed his eyes, and could almost forget the mud and the rain. Her old office building seemed to beckon so he walked over to the window and shaded his eyes and looked at her desk in the darkened room; the desk where she had worked all those years striving to give him a place to live, food to eat, clothing, and an education. Standing there by the window, he was sure she would come out of the other room and take her usual place at the desk, but he knew she was dead—and would never sit at that desk again. As he stood there, looking in the window at the darkened room where she had worked, he knew that the reason he wasn't back in Vietnam was because she was dead, and the reason she was dead was because he had left her alone and chose Vietnam over protecting her at home.

Leaving the window, he leaned back against a tree and watched the young girls walking past. Some smiled and their eyes were inviting. He wanted to celebrate life with them in ways he never understood before death had taken hold of his soul. They were blond, healthy, virginal...so different from the Vietnamese whores that were available in the villages, or the professional whores of Bangkok and Tijuana. 'Round eyes' he thought. They had referred to them as round-eyed pussy.

The last 'round eye' he had seen before Vietnam had been in Okinawa.

· · ·

A DESTINY OF MEMORIES

The troop carrier had docked there on Christmas Eve, and Marines were staggering back from a 24-hour dungaree liberty pass, the last liberty many would ever have; next stop Vietnam, death, maiming, and horror. She had auburn hair, much like Linda's, and her boyfriend, a USMC lieutenant was with her on the dock. He wondered who she was to have flown half way across the world to say one last goodbye to her Marine Lieutenant.

They kissed right there in front of a thousand silent Marines who were living the vicarious moment with them, and it was if she was kissing all of them—one last kiss. And then, some joker inflated a condom and let it fall from the ship's deck to the dock, where it danced in the breeze, and, to everyone's delight, landed on the young couple. The rest of the marines followed suit, and the sky was full of the torpedo like balloons falling on the couple who continued kissing, oblivious of anything but each other. Finally, they parted, and the Lieutenant grinned sheepishly at the wildly cheering marines, while kicking the inflated condoms aside as he walked up the gangplank. After all, what could they do? Send them to Vietnam?

• • •

He heard someone calling his name and turned around; it was Dennis, bearded, with bell-bottoms and a leather vest. There were two people with him. One he recognized as being a year or two younger than he was and the other a dark haired green-eyed girl somehow very familiar. He stared at her, all the time feeling something tugging at his heart. She returned his gaze, her green eyes seeming to swallow him whole. She had long auburn hair, minimum makeup and a low cut sweater that revealed a neckless which partly disappeared between her ample cleavage...a silver heart dangled from that chain.

Dennis didn't reach out to take his hand, or offer meaningless condolences; instead, he just smiled and asked, "If you aren't going anywhere special, why not join us at my place."

"I just buried my mother."

Dennis took his arm and the green-eyed girl took the other with the younger man following behind, "Come on. Let's go," Dennis said, "I didn't want to go to the funeral, too much of a bummer. I loved your mother, and didn't want to see her put in the ground."

Walking in step, they trucked down Main Street, and then turned left to the old Dunkirk Hub newspaper office. "We live upstairs. Old Harry Miedema rented us the place." Dennis said. "Let's go get a cup of coffee."

They sat on pillows spread out over the floor. The furniture was almost non-existent, so they placed the cups of coffee on the floor. Dennis lit a joint and they passed it around.

"You know what it's really all about, Dennis?" he asked and then qualified, "I mean...life."

"Life and death." Dennis echoed.

"Yeah, I guess what I really mean life and death." he agreed.

Dennis took a deep drag on the joint, waited, and let the smoke out, blowing little halos. He couldn't help but picture the Alice in Wonderland caterpillar sitting on the toadstool, "I believe something lives on after death..." Dennis seemed to be searching for the right word, and then instead gestured at the smoke, "Something like this smoke."

"I don't think so, Dennis," he said, "I've seen people die, and it's a fight for that last breath, and then, nothing...they die, just like any other animal, and that's it. Just nothingness. Black, nothing...no words...no comprehension. It's finally over."

"I believe that souls keep coming back until they lose their ego," Dennis blew more caterpillar smoke rings while attempting to stab his joint into the middle of one particularly large smoke ring continued, "and when they finish their many, many lives, they finally merge with the ALL. I suppose that would be a death of sorts, since all ego stops when they reach that higher existence. Life is only an ego trip after all is said and done."

The girl rolled over, and said, "You don't remember me, do you?" Her smile reminded him of his lost Linda, but then, right then everything seemed to remind him of something else.

"Sure I remember you." he lied.

"I'm sorry about your mother. I didn't know her very well, but whenever I went over to visit Pam, she was really nice to me. I read about you coming back in the paper. I'm Stella."

He remembered her now, a short but very well proportioned Greek girl with green eyes, remarkable in this town of big blue-eyed Norwegian girls many nearly six feet tall.

"You tried to pick me up before you left. I didn't like you very much then, but now..." she smiled, "now maybe I feel differently."

"You thought I said something insulting. I don't even remember what it was."

"You're forgiven if you take me home. I live just outside of town on Highway 51 across from the hatchery."

"When?"

She stretched like a cat preparing to pounce. She had been jailbait back then, but now she was fair game.

"Right now! You *do* have a car?"

"Yeah," he said, "but we have to walk a ways since I left it down by the Highway Trailer Plant."

"Cool." she purred.

"I'm leaving now," he turned to Dennis, "and thanks for the joint and the coffee."

Dennis shrugged and half-waved as they walked out the door, down the stairs and back into the street. He was high but he had learned that he functioned a lot better with pot than booze. In Vietnam, some of the guys preferred Jack Daniels, but it left them a little lethargic, and the pot was far better. They walked together arm in arm, back up Main Street.

'They know so little of death and even less of life.' he thought. He had seen too many men die...they all either called for their mothers, or God, or Jesus, but if they were lucky, a corpsman or a buddy would hold them trying to keep the poor marine alive a little longer...pressing bandages into gaping wounds, trying to keep the life-blood from flowing out...and for nothing. They would all die sooner or later and join the waiting heroes in the land of the dead.

Walking with this green eyed Greek girl, arm in arm, he searched the faces of the people coming out of the shops, or just strolling, some holding hands, and for brief moments their eyes would meet his, and then quickly look away as if eye contact with him was an invasion of his privacy. While he didn't know or recognize these people, he was sure some at least knew him by sight. A violent death in a small Wisconsin town was great grist for the local gossip mills. So, he silently challenged them to break eye contact first, and when they did, was satisfied with that small victory. He put his arm around Stella's waist letting his hand slip down to feel her muscular thigh as he felt her hand slip into his back pocket.

He grinned down at her, "Hey, the wallets in the other pocket."

She gave him a playful squeeze and boldly smiled back, "I'm not interested in your wallet...this time."

When they arrived at the car, he opened the door for her. Something about Stella seemed to command that kind of attention. On the way to her home, she told him about the small town things that mattered to her.

"I was surprised that you smoke grass." Stella said.

"Why?"

"I mean, you never used to be the type," then she paused, "and people talk about soldiers who come back. You've changed. People notice. You were such a square, I mean, you didn't go out for sports, you never got into trouble, but now, you seem...dangerous."

Not knowing what to say he just nodded and said, "Great. Do I frighten you?"

She grinned and said, "Should I be? It turns me on." And then she asked, "What were the girls like, over there?"

He smiled, "Well, up in the mountains they chewed betel nut root and their teeth were usually black from it by the time they hit age 14. In the cities, like Hue, lots of then were part French and Chinese, and they were very graceful."

"Did you have anyone? I mean, you know...were you with them?"

He laughed and saw that she was a bit offended so stopped, "Stella, the only women we saw were either the enemy soldiers shooting at us or diseased whores. We kept away from both as much as possible. Those that didn't...well some of the guys never came home, and what they caught you don't want to know about."

They pulled up to her home; a farmhouse with a small barn, which had been converted into a workshop. "Don't drive in," she said, "it's best if my step-dad doesn't see you bringing me home."

He gave her a look, "It's complicated." she explained. Then she impulsively reached over and kissed him long and deep. She broke away and said, "That's so you remember me until the next time." She got out of the car and ran up the driveway, looking back once, to grin at him.

He liked the feel of the kiss and driving back to his grandmothers, he felt somehow lighter. As soon as he walked in the door, she poured him the usual Norwegian greeting cup of coffee and asked if he wanted anything else. "Mercedes and Eldorae were here for a while, but they couldn't wait. Eldorae had to get back to Chicago and Mercedes went back to the Dells. They both said you could stay with them if you want."

"No, I don't think so."

"I wouldn't want to stay with them either." she sipped her coffee, dunked an Oreo Cookie, took a bite of the now soggy treat and said; "Wally and Hazel would like you to take their son's old room. They fixed it up and sometimes rent it to bachelor teachers in the high school. They say it's pretty nice, has its own bathroom and a side entrance. A lot better than that old cot and the bathroom down the hall that we have here, and having to sharing it with three other families."

"Maybe your right Grandma. I have to store a few things anyway and it's pretty crowded here with me taking up what little room you have."

"Gotta be practical," she said, "and anyway they loved your mother and it would make them feel good to have you stay there."

"Ok. Call and tell them I'll move in tomorrow." he was tired. Every bone in his body ached. He could feel the glue that had held him together during the long trip from Vietnam begin to dissolve and he wearily lay down on the cot in the alcove. "I just need a few hours' sleep," he said.

"I'll call Wally and Hazel then. Get some rest Tim."

He closed his eyes, and heard the Simon Sisters on a neighbor's radio. They were singing "Motherless Child" and he was still a long, long way from home.

CHAPTER 6

He woke to the early morning sounds of his Grandmother frying the usual salt pork and making her thick black coffee. She would use the grease, add a little butter, and burn some eggs to go with it. He stretched, gave her a good morning, and walked down the hall to the small communal bathroom. After Vietnam, this was a luxury rather than a hardship but everyone seemed to think he would be better off staying with the Netterblad's, so he had agreed.

It was still too early to stop by their house, and anyway, it was Sunday and they were Church People and wouldn't be home until after the services were over. They had attended the Lutheran Church for years, possibly because it was located a few hundred yards from their two-story red brick home. So he loaded his kit bag and a few things into the VW's trunk (located in the front, the engine being in the back were trunks were supposed to be) and then returned to his Grandmother's apartment to say goodbye.

"Hazel Netterblad called while you were out. They would like to invite you for Sunday dinner."

"I guess I can't get out of it." She gave him one of her looks.

"Ok, ok. I'll go. I have to pick up some more things from the house first."

He drove through the town...nothing was open except Friedman's general store, since as a Jew, Friedman didn't have to obey the local "blue laws"; a fact greatly appreciated by the locals when they stopped by after Church to purchase groceries, milk or anything else that they had run short of. The grocery stores, businesses, and taverns were closed. Only the gas stations, restaurants, and Friedman's General Store stayed open. Dunkirk was a farming community that functioned as a hub for the surrounding farms. The farm-folk, dressed in their Sunday best, would mingle with the city-folk in the churches, which numbered only slightly less than the taverns. After prayers, they would stop at Friedman's general store, or maybe have a hearty dinner at Violet's restaurant, then one more stop to gas up, and back to a quiet Sunday watching sports on TV until it would be time for the evening chores.

The taverns wouldn't open until sundown. He wondered why they just didn't wait until Monday to let the bars re-open, but the law said closed until sundown. Once he asked his mother why this was and she shrugged and said that it had always been that way.

Spitting on the sidewalk was also an offense and he remembered when some of his friends had tried it out in front of Percy, the Chief of Police, just to see what would happen. They were hauled in to the station; their parents notified and forced to pay a fine to get them released. However, before he arrested them, they were forced to clean the spit from the sidewalk on their hands and knees, as Percy stood over them, a hand resting on the butt of his service revolver, which almost disappeared under the folds of Percy's great stomach.

He drove over the Main Street Bridge, turned left on South Page, and then stopped in front of the house. Back in the 30s, she was living with her Uncle Ben and Aunt Dora above the tavern. Ben came home one morning and told them he had won a house in his latest poker game, he was a professional gambler and played high stakes poker for most of his life. They moved from the apartment above the tavern on Sixth Street and, until the house was lost in another poker game some years later, she spent most of her high school years there. It was more respectable than living above the family tavern and was certainly a lot quieter.

Walking up the short cement sidewalk that led to the front porch he almost opened the front door, then paused, and decided to knock. Pam walked down the stairs, across room, opened the door, and invited him in.

"Thanks for coming around and to see me," she said. He detected a trace of sarcasm in her voice.

"Where's your father?" he asked.

"They took him to the VA hospital after the funeral. He was talking crazy and my Aunt got him into rehab, at Mendota," she hesitated and then went on, "it's not the first time." Mendota was the state mental hospital.

"What are you going to do now?"

She walked over to the couch and sat with both hands clenched together resting on her knees. "I thought I told you, I'm going to live with my Aunt. They're closing this place down and after the auction are putting it up for sale. It's an estate thing." There were blank spaces in his memory, and the last few days were like a blur.

"An estate thing. An auction." he echoed and sat beside her.

She turned to him and he could see the tears beginning to well in her eyes. "There's nothing I could do, Tim. Everything was left to Dad and my Aunt is handling the estate now that he isn't functional. The last thing Dad did after your Mom...died...was to give her full power of attorney and now it's her decision, so she is selling everything as soon as possible."

"So..." he couldn't hide the bitterness in his voice, "nothing for me." The picture of his former friends and neighbors pawing everything, looking for sales, buying everything that might have connected him to his past, disgusted him.

She reached out and put her hand on his, "Not even the VW. I got her to agree to let you use it until you go back to Vietnam, but since you signed it over to your Mom before you left, it became a part of the estate."

Removing her hand he said, "I'll be taking some things before the vultures descend to inventory everything...some clothes, my spare kit bag, and as many of the family albums as I can carry."

She nodded in agreement. "You're right; they haven't taken an inventory yet so just take whatever you can. I'll help you pack and carry things out to the VW. I think we have some cold beer, would you like one?" She ground out a cigarette butt and immediately lit a second.

"No, no thanks." he said, watching her light another cigarette, which that reminded him he needed a smoke too. "Hey, I don't have a lighter—give me a pig fuck?"

He took her cigarette and used it to light up his Marlboro. She noticed that his hand trembled and so reached out to steady it with hers. In spite of the gesture, there remained a silence between them, solid and impenetrable. He couldn't open up. To open up was to get hurt and he already hurt enough.

"I thought we might throw a party tonight, "she said, "You know, sort of a welcome home so you can get a chance to see a few of your old friends."

"You mean the ones that aren't in the 'Nam or haven't already come home in body bags." It wasn't a question; just a bitter fact and he could tell she was unhappy that he mentioned it.

"Not everyone went to Vietnam," she said, "and not everyone died there."

"Pam, everyone died in the 'Nam. Some of us just don't know it yet."

"Finish your smoke," she said, "I'm going upstairs and start packing for you. Actually, I have to pack for me too. I'll probably be out of here soon enough."

He no longer wanted the cigarette and crushed it violently into the ashtray. He was about to get up when the phone rang. It continued ringing and finally, in exasperation, he answered it, "Yeah."

"Tim?" he recognized the voice. It was Linda. "Tim, how are you?" she said.

He didn't feel friendly and answered, "What do you want, Linda."

He could hear her breathing and a finally she said, "I wanted to explain." When he remained silent, she went on, "I wanted to wait for you, but I went out. It was only one time, but...it was enough. I got pregnant." She waited for him to answer but he knew all about silences. "Tim, are you there?" she asked.

"Yeah."

"My Mom made us get married in the Church. I never told you but I got pregnant once before—I was 15. I wanted an abortion but—good Catholic girls don't do that. My mom made me have the baby, then she took it away from me, and my baby son went to someone else...I don't even know to whom. When I got pregnant again...I needed to keep this one, so I married the guy, and then he got drafted and they sent him over there."

"Do you love him?" he asked.

"I love you. I want to divorce him and then we can still be together."
He listened to the words but even if he still loved her it didn't matter any
longer, nothing mattered, so he remained silent and just listened to her
breathing on the line. Her husband was fighting in Vietnam and she was
offering herself to him here and now...back in The World. It made him
realize that some things are better left dead...it was time to find
someone else.

"Good bye Linda. You forgot one thing; Catholics don't believe in
divorce so I hope he makes it back. If he doesn't your problem is solved.
You won't need a divorce and you'll have that $10,000 dollar GI Insurance
to keep you warm at night." he hung up.

After a few moments, the phone began to ring again. He let it ring
until Pam picked up the extension upstairs. He could hear her speaking,
and then she hung up, and came downstairs.

"You knew she was calling."

"Yes," she had tears in her eyes, "Linda wanted to make it all right
with you."

"Congratulations, Pam. Linda is as dead to me as my mother. I
suppose you listened in and that was Linda who called back."

She nodded.

"Ok. Let's start over. We have packing to do and I have to start
shopping for another car."

"And the party?" she asked.

"Sure. Set it up. Oh, and invite Stella."

She seemed surprised, "She's not good enough for you Tim."

He laughed, "Yeah. Not like Linda who wants to get rid of her
husband fighting in the 'Nam and get some shack up time with me
before I go back."

"It's over with Linda then?" she asked.

"It's over," he answered, "she's married and pregnant by a soldier
fighting for a fucking country that doesn't give a damn about him. She's
already forgotten him just as she forgot me, just as all of you have
forgotten us. I guess that's just the way you are and the way I am, so
fucking forget it and bring me a beer."

She brought two beers and passed one to him. "Don't you think I know what she did...what she is," she sipped her beer, "and what we all are. You must hate all of us."

Her sadness was real and once again, he felt bad for dumping on this little girl who might have been a sister to him. "Look Pam. I'm sorry for some of the things I said. I don't have anything left inside. Everything that I had—everything I was—it's gone now, and I came home only to find out that there isn't anything to come home to...or for."

"I didn't mean any harm, Tim. I would never hurt you; we both have had too much pain already. Right now, I don't even know what's going to happen to me. My dad was talking crazy when my Aunt took him away. He feels responsible and it landed him back in the psych ward. So now, I have to move in with Linda and my Aunt. I was hoping—that is I wanted to see if you and Linda could...but no, that's over. We're never going to be a family, are we?"

"No," he said, "never."

"Well at least that bitch cousin of mine didn't destroy you," she said, "Linda would like nothing better than to cheat on her husband and get together with you and then probably dump you if he makes it back."

"That's sounds like Linda." he raised his beer bottle in a mock toast to his past love. "I can't be hurt anymore Pam, not now and not ever. I'm a survival expert and plan to outlive, outfox, and outlast everything they throw at me, and the reason is because nothing matters."

She lifted her beer in a toast, "So here's to the party and to Stella and to you having a good time, and fuck Linda."

"Fuck Linda!" he agreed as they touched glasses. "I'll drink to that little Sister and to this: In the land of the night the chariot of the sun is drawn by the grateful dead." he downed the beer.

She looked at him and shivered, "You're creeping me out Big Brother!"

"The Book of the Dead." he said as the full verse echoed in his mind: 'As they stand at the edge of darkness, let their chant fill the void so people would know that in the land of darkness the chariot of Sun is drawn by the grateful dead.'

He went upstairs and helped her finish packing. 'So this is all I have left', he thought. 'A kitbag, scraps of some uniforms, and the Marie

Corps'. Those two kit bags and some money in the bank were all that remained of his worldly possessions. From here on, he would travel lite and it would be a lone, lonely way.

She walked him to the VW where he popped the trunk, loaded the bags, and then turned to her.

"See you tonight?" she asked.

"Sure," he smiled, "should be a lot of fun."

He drove to Netterblad's home and off-loaded his bags in John's room, then went downstairs. They had returned from Church and the delicious smells of a traditional Sunday Dinner drifted in from the kitchen. He sat with Wally in their living room.

"You can stay here for as long as you like, Tim." Wally was a Swiss national with US Citizenship, a medium built man his signature close trimmed mustache being his most prominent feature; a man who had taught printing at the High School and had lived in Dunkirk since the end of WWII. In the war, he had served with distinction in England in the Red Cross during the Blitz. Wally's eyes were red from weeping and he sat disconsolately in the armchair.

"Leo dragged her down, down, down," he said, "and then...well the police will investigate what happened. Leo killed her, Tim—he took her from us."

"I heard Leo was admitted to the psychiatric hospital in Mendota," he said, trying to change the subject.

"Sooner or later they will have to release him, and then..." Wally wrung his hands, "and then he will pay for killing her."

"Did he kill her?" he asked.

Wally looked up and there was anger in his eyes, "Leo killed her, it doesn't matter how—he's responsible."

Hazel Netterblad came in, "Enough talk gentlemen. Come and sit down."

As soon as he saw the table with its variety of spoons, forks, and knives, he felt totally out of place. For months, he had been eating what was available with either fingers or plastic forks. Everything had been in cold C-ration cans, except for an occasional chance to visit a base mess hall, where the food was mostly the same, but warmer. The C-Rats came in a case containing 12 meals. Each meal was in its own cardboard box, which contained the individual items sealed in cans. A can opener (called both a 'John Wayne' and a 'P-38') was needed to open the cans. Some of the meals weren't too bad when semi heated with the little "Sterno" bar provided ("Fuel Tablet, Ration Heating"), especially if somebody from home sent Heinz-57 Sauce or Hot Sauce to doctor them up. Others were downright awful (Ham and Lima beans called 'ham and mothafuckers) were usually passed over—left behind for the 'boots' when it was their turn to pick out meals. His squad tried to keep it fair and would dump the case of C-Rats upside down (hiding the name of the meal) and mix it up to give everyone an equal chance of selecting a popular meal.

Sitting in their dining room, he was amazed to see serving platters of beef, chicken, pork, mashed potatoes, and gravy...enough to feed his entire squad. All of it steaming and making his mouth water.

Noticing his uneasiness Wally assured him, "Don't worry about the silverware, just take what you want, and use what you want to eat it with," he smiled and indicated the feast with his hand. "You lost a lot of weight, and we're going to change that starting today."

Wally took his plate and filled it with mountains of everything. He tried to eat slowly, but couldn't resist tearing into the feast like the starving animal that he was. During the meal, he had stuffed, not bothering to open a conversation, and Hazel Netterblad looked on in shocked silence as he ate the chicken with his fingers.

Holding his hand over his mouth, he belched, pushed the chair away from the table, and said, "That was great. I haven't eaten like this in a long time."

On the 4th of July, someone back in HQ (Head Quarters) had ordered a couple of crates of stakes and beer helicoptered to them at their forward base camp. No one waited for medium rare or well done and instead tore into the bloody meat as soon as it was warm, washing it down with hot sun-warmed beer.

Mrs. Netterblad cleared the table as Wally led him to the living room where he gratefully sank into the soft cushions.

"Did you go to church?" Wally asked.

"No," he answered truthfully. "I don't believe in it anymore."

Wally considered this for a moment and then leaned forward and said in a hushed tone not intended for his wife to hear, "Confidentially Tim, I don't blame you. The things you must have seen...but it's over now. I'm pushing to get you stationed stateside."

"Thank you, but it really doesn't matter much to me. This emergency leave is only for another two weeks, and then I go back." he wasn't sure that he wanted to stay in the states. There was nothing here for him now. "At least in the Marines we know where we stand and who has our backs."

"I want you to feel at home here." Wally was sincere, the man had tears in his eyes, "I owe it to your mother to try and change that for you. You are all there is left of her."

He looked around the living room. There was an oversized picture of their son John in an explorer scouts uniform, with a sash overflowing with merit badge accomplishments. John had visited him when he finished boot camp in San Diego. After moving to San Diego when he finished Law school, John had bought a small house on the hill that overlooked that little patch of hell called San Diego boot camp. On graduation day they were allowed visitors and John came down to say hello...after a long and strained silence, John left, and he, not having any other relatives or friends visiting, walked back to the Quonset hut and packed his kit bag for his transfer to ITR (Infantry Training Regiment). Now, looking at the picture, and sleeping in John's bed, he began to realize why he too had traveled so far from home and its stifling environment. Too much possessive love, he thought, just as his own mother had tried to possess him. The Marine Corps was his escape, and practicing law in San Diego was John's way out.

"I won't rest until that...bastard is behind bars." Wally said, "So don't do anything foolish. Don't take it into your own hands."

He smiled and said, "All I want to do is go up to the room and sack out...that was a great feast, and I really appreciate all you are doing for me." He excused himself and went upstairs, flushed the toilet a few times just to watch the water go down, and again marveled at how such a simple thing could seem like an unexpected luxury. Then he stretched out on the bed and studied the ceiling cracks until he nodded off.

• • •

There were three of them, in an "L" shaped rifle pit that had half filled with water as the monsoon rains continued to fall. The temperature was barely above freezing, but it felt much lower since they'd been wet even before they moved into their defensive position for the night, and now, sitting belly deep in muddy water, the chill made his soaked legs so numb that he couldn't feel the silver dollar sized leaches that were stealthily fastening themselves to his body. He knew they were there...they were always there.

Behind them was the Phu Bai airfield. Most of the aircraft were grounded because of the constant rain, mist, and fog. The croaking of the frogs and the mosquitos were the only things keeping them company except for the 155mm illumination rounds that cast eerie shadows over the landscape as they slowly descended on their parachutes; momentarily making the constant mind numbing drizzle of the monsoon rain visible. Then, without warning, the entire tree line on the other side of the rice paddy lit up as the VC set off trip flares. They were under fire and mortars began to walk their deadly way from the perimeter toward the airfield. VC sappers and infantry began to splash through the paddy moving swiftly toward their fighting hole. The field telephone rang and the order was short and concise, "Fix bayonets and open fire!"

He squeezed the firing mechanism of the claymore[10] mines they had planted and he took satisfaction as he watched them shred the first wave of VC.

• • •

---

[10] Designed to counter human-wave assaults, the Claymore uses a shaped C-4 charge to fire several hundred steel balls into a designated 55-yard killing zone.

He woke and focused his eyes on the cracks in the ceiling, fought the trembling of his hands, and pulled himself into a sitting position. He had slept the afternoon away and it was getting dark. There was a foul taste in his mouth and the sweat clung to his body. He staggered into the bathroom, stripped, and stood in the shower, letting the scalding water wash away the memories. In the 'Nam hot water was as much of a luxury as flush toilets, cold drinks, and a bed to sleep in. He looked at himself in the full-length mirror as he toweled dry. The person looking back at him was older, thinner, and stooped over with an infantryman's hump. He straightened up feeling the bones in his back crack in protest. Months of humping in the boonies had left him stooped from the weight of his field marching pack, spare c-rations and ammo—the permanent humped back of the Marine grunt. His body was scarred from various Band-Aid wounds but he was alive and in the states and going out to party.

He needed a smoke, but there were no ashtrays in the house. The Netterblads neither smoked nor drank anything stronger than a glass of wine on Christmas. He lit a cigarette and retired to the bathroom where he sat on the toilet and flicked his ashes into the sink. Finishing the cigarette, he "field stripped" the filter by ripping it into its component parts, wrapped it in toilet paper, and flushed. The room smelled of smoke and he felt guilty, then dressed and walked down the stairs, which led to his private entrance. Pausing by the door leading to the living room, he opened it, stuck his head in and seeing Wally sitting in his easy chair still reading the Sunday paper, he said, "I'm going to visit some friends and might not be back until late. I'll try to be as quiet as possible."

Was he asking for permission? But Wally simply nodded and said, "Have a good time. Our doors are always open."

It was a relief to leave the house. For many years, he had tended their garden; shoveled the snow from their sidewalk, and did the odd jobs that John had done before he escaped. He knew that in their eyes he was the same 18-year-old boy that had left to serve his country and he also knew he didn't belong, not in their house, nor in the town...and possibly not in this world that continued in its daily routine while his friends were fighting and dying. He felt like someone who had crossed a suspension bridge attached from one side of a cliff to the other that had collapsed leaving him stranded on the other side, looking back at a world to which he could never go back.

'It doesn't matter.' he thought. 'Nothing matters. Only way to go now is forward.'

It was evening and the town was beginning to wake up from the daylong slumber of the Wisconsin Sabbath. The bars were opening and as he drove down the street, he felt an urge to stop in to the bowling alley and start the evening with a beer. The old alley, where the pin boys would work after school hand setting the pins, had gone out of business when the new fully automated Badger Lanes had opened next to the Main Street Bridge. There were 12 lanes and during his high school years, it was the place to be. The bar was separated from the alleys by a glass partition, and served anyone over 18.

Families would come and while the kids bowled, the parents would have a few beers and sit watching them from behind the glass windows. There was a window where soft drinks and burgers could be purchased and brought back to the tables that matched the colored plastic crescent shaped benches that faced each alley.

The alleys were empty, only a few bowlers had arrived, and he didn't recognize anyone so he continued into the bar where he ordered a beer and sat watching the bowlers.

"Hey Tim!"

He turned and looked at the big man standing behind him. The face looked familiar, "Rich—it's been a long time." Rich sank into the barstool.

"Sure has, Tim. I haven't seen you since we graduated from High School. Let me buy you another one." He motioned to the barkeep, held up two fingers, and indicated the empty mug on the bar. The bartender carefully filled two large ones and slid them toward them. They caught the thick mugs of cold Wisconsin Beer before they stopped moving, raised them in a mock salute, clinked glasses, and locked eyes as they chugged it down waiting to see who would win the contest of being first to finish without taking a breath, then slammed their empty glasses down on the bar, belched loudly, and ordered two more.

"Jesus Christ you look like shit, Tim. Sorry about your Mom...I hear you were in Vietnam when they told you about her."

He stared at the bubbles in his glass. "Yeah. I was in the 'Nam when they told me."

Rich held up his right hand, a finger was missing. "I got a deferment for this. Caught it in a machine at the Rubber plant and the gears didn't leave much left. Lucky it wasn't my hand. Anyway, they rejected me at the draft board."

"You're lucky Rich—damn lucky. Sometimes I wish I'd stayed in school and never joined up."

"Are the bastards sending you back?" Rich took a long sip of his beer and reached for the free hard-boiled eggs, dipped one in a small bowl of salt, and finished it in one bite.

"I don't know. I'm staying at the Netterblad's until I get my shit together. The old man says he might have the pull to keep me stateside, but don't know if I want to stay. Nothing feels right. I mean, I've had it with Vietnam, but all this..." he swung his beer in a 180-degree crescent, "all this doesn't feel right. I don't belong here."

"Pretty rough over there?"

"Yeah." he continued gazing into his beer. They were both silent for a while.

"I hope they get you out of going back, Tim." Rich's voice was both sincere and concerned, "You've done enough—been through enough. Let's have another round." he said, and slapped a dollar on the counter.

After he quit the University and before enlisting in the Marines, he had worked at the U.S. Rubber factory with Rich on the graveyard shift. There had been a fire. The smoke was so thick that the only thing he could make out was Rich, with those big hands of his, reaching out and dragging him to an exit. He remembered thinking that if he had to die, let it be for something worthwhile, not as an hourly wageworker in a stink-hole of a factory, each eight-hour shift just a small part of an endless life waiting to reach retirement age; the day after the fire, he had taken a bus to Madison, walked into the Marine Corps recruiting office, and signed up.

"Go back to school, Tim. Take the GI Bill and make something of yourself. You always were a "brain" in High School, and going back to school and getting paid for it from Uncle Sam isn't the worst thing in the world," he smiled, "and for guys like me, working at the Rubber is as good as it gets. A hundred bucks a week, plenty of overtime and maybe get married someday...buy a house, and start a family. Hell yes, let's drink to that!"

He was starting to feel the effects of the beer. The beer tasted better than he remembered. Good beer and bad thoughts vied for control. In the end, the memories won out—memories that had once been good and now hurt him like a kick to the stomach. His Mother wrote him to ask if he was afraid. He didn't know how to answer her letter. Fear had become so commonplace it had become a part of him, and once fear settles in, it becomes something different—adrenaline addiction. He had become an action-junkie, and even now, back in the "world" he felt the need to keep moving. By the fifth beer, he could feel her again, not dead in the grave, but somehow sitting next to him on the empty stool.

• • •

The river and the cemetery hadn't freed him from her after all. On the cold, wet dark days of winter—the limbo days where it was too warm for snow and the world was grey with sleet, it was then that she would play the piano for hours while he sat on the carpeted floor with his toy soldiers fighting mock battles, which would become real ones far too soon. The piano was out of tune, and it annoyed him. From time to time, she would turn her head and watch him play and she would smile that special smile of hers which was both warm and bittersweet. It was at times like that he felt she was trying to reach out and share her secrets, but she never did—she died and took them with her, leaving nothing behind but memories and betrayal.

• • •

"You're dead," he mumbled to her.
    "Say what?"

98

"Sorry just thinking out loud. Let's have another beer and maybe afterwards you might want to party before you start the night shift. My stepsister Pam is having a few people over, sort of a cross between a welcome home for me and a wake for my mom."

Rich smiled that big generous smile of his. "Hey, I'm always up for a party. If I get soused enough won't even notice the stink at the plant."

They finished their beers and got in their cars. He followed Rich being careful to stay within the speed limit since he was clearly fair game for any cop that would happily pull him over and write him a ticket for drunk driving.

This time he didn't knock, just opened the door and walked in. Pam had cold beers ready for them. People filtered in, but while the faces were familiar, he didn't know them all by name. They were mostly Pam's friends. He sat back in the over-stuffed easy chair and chugged his beer. Stella came out of the kitchen with two more beers and sat on the armrest. She gave him a wicked smile and slipped down on top of him, snuggling into his lap. Her body was warm and real and he slipped one arm around her as she pressed into him, placing one hand on his thigh, moving it teasingly up and then down his leg. Rich sat next to Pam on the couch and they talked quietly for a while, then Rich winked at him and pulled Pam closer.

People came and left, some bringing six packs while others discretely went into the kitchen to smoke joints. Stella didn't bother being discrete, she just lit up a joint and passed it to him. He inhaled deeply, passed it back, and felt himself drifting, nodding off from time to time, as the music and the familiar yet not familiar faces seemed to blur. Pam was still sitting on the couch but Rich had disappeared. "Where's Rich?" he asked.

"He had to go to work. He said to say goodbye for him." Stella nuzzled his ear.

"Oh." he was drunk and high and couldn't remember Rich leaving. The room seemed to shift and the shadows caused by the low wattage bulbs lengthened. Someone sat next to Pam. His hair was short, and the sidewalls identified him as a Marine back home from boot camp. The Marine looked over and gave him a thumbs up. "I hear you're a marine just back from Vietnam. *Semper fi.*" he said and sipped his beer,

"Yeah."

"I'll be going there soon," he added, "and maybe you can tell me what's it's like."

"You're the Benson kid from that big dairy farm just off highway 51, right?"

"Yeah," he nodded.

"Well Benson it's like this. Being over there is like being in a car wreck and not knowing if you are going to live through it. Your nerves will be shot after the first three months on Patrol, and you'll hate the rain in winter and curse the dust in summer. If you're lucky you might get malaria and be sent home. If you aren't lucky they'll send you home in a bag...hell, they'll even put whatever can find of your body parts in that same bag, or if the pieces are small, they stick them in a separate bag...but don't worry your name and serial number will be clearly stenciled on both bags so when it's time to plant you in the ground, you'll be more or less complete. Nobody left behind...not even pieces."

•   •   •

He closed his eyes and relived the night and the monsoon, when a Claymore had misfired, and Tom crawled on his belly into the rice paddy to reattach the wire. Someone had stepped on the plunger before he got back, and in the morning, they formed a line, policed the area looking for more body parts, placing them in a bag, and then passing again and again over the kill zone until there wasn't anything left to find.

•   •   •

"But don't worry, Benson, when death comes you'll never hear the shot that takes your life. It is one of the few blessings of war."

The room became quiet and the kids stopped dancing and looked at him as if he was insane. He realized that he was raising his voice. "Yeah...body bagged back to the good old US of A where you get dumped into a hole and forgotten about. *Semper fi!*" he said raising his bottle in a toast and the bitterness in his own voice surprised him.

"I won't be like you, Tim." Benson said.

He dared the boy to lock eyes and after what seemed like an eternity, Benson looked away, and then he gave the young Marine his best advice, "Become like me as fast as you can, or you're a dead man walking. Some of you last a month or two, and then you get cocky...after cocky comes careless and then you either get yourself or your buddies killed or, if you don't get your shit together, they'll do the job for the VC and frag[11] your silly ass."

His eyes seemed to grow larger and he stuttered incredulously, "You'd kill your own men?"

He took a long swig, "We call it self-defense...if it's your life or mine well—'Xin Loi', or translated into English: 'sorry 'bout that shit.'"

Stella whispered, "Tim, I think you should cool it."

Benson seemed to digest this and then in a voice that seemed more sorrowful than accusatory went on, "What happened to you, Tim. What happened over there? You were so gung-ho before you left."

Sobered a bit by the sincerity of the question he leaned forward, not caring that he had become the center of attention and said, "We believed in the theories, in the danger to America, and the whole thing that they taught us in High school since the Missile crises. At first you go there feeling righteous...like joining a crusade, trained and ready to go, gung-ho, for God, Corps, and Country. After a while in country, you stop including God and country and the only thing that remains is Corps. Your friends die, mistakes are made, and in the end, you forget about Corps too...the only thing that matters is the grunt standing at your side or covering your ass and you god dammed better cover his. The life over there consists of mud, fear, and suffering; killing little kids that should never be holding their AK-47s. Those little kids still believe in what they fight for...to throw us out of their shitty little rice paddies and crummy huts. They have no idea where America is, or why we came to their homes, all they know is we are invading their life and they fight to the death to get rid of us. Hell, they don't even know what communism is. You've forgotten us in your world of parties, school, and good times. The lucky ones will get a deferment, the rest of you, working class guys, will be drafted and most of you will die, or wish you were dead before it's over. Benson, I wish you well but odds are you will finish your tour in a body bag." He opened another beer, "I've said enough. *Semper fi* and get the hell out of my face, boot."

He heard the words 'coward', and 'burned-out' being whispered and then people started leaving the party.

---

[11] Frag: the M-26 fragmentation grenade. Fragging, used for assassination of an unpopular member of one's own fighting unit

Benson shook his head and walked out, and he thought he saw Pam take someone upstairs, and then closed his eyes for what might have been a few minutes or even an hour. It felt good, sitting next to Stella, her head on his shoulder, and he allowed himself to dream a futile dream of what might have been.

Stella was talking to him. "Pam went upstairs with a guy and it's been a long time. Don't you think you should do something?"

He was suddenly very tired, "What should I do?"

"I know the guy she left with. He's bad news and is probably raping her." Stella said.

"Kill him!" someone piped up.

"You say that word so easily." he looked around the room. "Be my guest." he motioned to the stair. When nobody moved, he sighed in disgust, "Figured not. It's over. Not much of a party anyway. I'm out of here." He pulled himself out of the easy chair and Stella steadied him as they walked out to the car where Stella guided him to the passenger seat, held out her hand, and ordered, "Keys!"

He smiled, fished in his pocket, and handed them to her as she said, "You can't go back to Netterblad's in your state...they'd throw you out for sure. I know a place we can crash for the night."

She drove and he nodded off. The heater felt good on his legs and he leaned on her shoulder closing his eyes as his head rested against her perfumed neck.

• • •

The Brass had given him R&R in Bangkok after the attack on the airfield. When he arrived at the hotel, the first thing he did was go to the international telephone center. There was just one way to call out of Thailand, and that meant waiting in turn to get a booth for international calls. The papers were full of the action of the war in Israel. Most of the people ahead of him were Israelis, so he had asked them whom they were calling. One of them, a reserve paratrooper who spoke perfect English told him that they were calling their units and trying to get back to join the fight. When they found out that he was a Marine on R&R from Vietnam an instant bond was formed, addresses were exchanged, and promises were made. One of them gave up his place in line, and he had five precious minutes to speak with his mother...the last time he would ever hear her voice. She said she was happy and that they had bought the house. When he came home, they would be a real family. She promised to send him a few hundred dollars via western union. He asked if everything was ok, and she assured him that Leo was working at the airport and things they're going well. His time was up, and he reluctantly gave the phone to the next in line.

• • •

"Wake up, we're here." It was Dennis' place. "Don't worry, if he isn't in I have a key. We can crash here tonight."

"And your parents?"

"They think I'm spending the night at a girl friend's house," she gave him her wicked smile again, "like you say about your Marines, we girls cover for each other too."

He was feeling better now, and followed her up the stairs to Dennis' apartment. They knocked, but there was no answer. She sighed and opened the door. The room smelled of incense, obviously to cover the telltale odor of pot. No one was home. She led him to a waterbed. They sat down and she played the sound track from "the good, the bad, and the Ugly" which had become popular after he shipped out to Vietnam, and smoked a small pipe of hash then she stripped and urgently undressed him. They lay quietly together, listing to the music and enjoying the mutual warmth of their bodies. Then she slipped on top of him and gently, and with great tenderness, they made love.

He lost himself in her arms and the world, Vietnam, his mother's death and the town was eclipsed by the warmth and joy of loving and being loved in return. Afterward they slept in each other's arms, time stopped, and exhaustion and release caused him to fall into a deep and dreamless sleep.

CHAPTER 7

He awoke with a throbbing head and shivered uncontrollably. Although still under the blankets, his body felt cold—drained. He reached out for Stella but she was gone. When he attempted to stand up the room seemed to be rolling like a ship at sea, so he sat on a straight-backed chair next to Dennis' dilapidated heavily stained worktable on which he created his masterpieces. There was a note. He opened it and with great effort managed to focus his eyes. The note was from Dennis:

'Stella left early (that's Stella, get used to it, she comes and goes). Help yourself to whatever little there is. The coffee I made yesterday is still probably drinkable so feel free. I'll be at the University today. I'll see you when I see you.'

His orders were to report to the USMC and Naval reserve depot on University Avenue after the funeral, and he knew that it would be a good idea for him to report in. Besides, he wanted to see the University and the Rat (Rathskeller) and maybe find a familiar face or two. The Rat, a famous U.W. landmark, was located on the first floor of the Memorial Union, and it had been one of his favorite places to hang out, drink coffee, and listen to music.

Seeing the nasty mold in Dennis' coffee cups made the decision easy for him...better to wait on the coffee, so he locked the door on the way out, leaving the key where they found it. Coffee would wait. It was still early and traffic was lite on Highway 51 so within 40 minutes he had already found a parking place on Langdon Street. He listened to "good vibrations" on the radio and Linda crept unwanted into his mind, and so he countered with thoughts of Stella, but knew that this entire time with her was little more than R&R not unlike the time he spent in Bangkok, but this time no exchange of money for services was involved.

The trees were already shedding their leaves, fading just as his world had, and soon the bare branches would stand in stark contrast to the cold winter skies; their sleeping bodies sometimes covered with snow or glistening with a glass-like coating of ice, a reminder of what was, yet, still a slumbering promise of what might be when spring eventually returns. Walking to the Student Union, he observed that the mode of dress had changed, skirts were much shorter, but here on the campus they were scarce since everyone seemed to be sporting navy peacoats or army field jackets with bell-bottoms.

He opened the massive doors to the first floor, walked down the long hallway, and then turned right into the Rathskeller. Gone were the clean-cut students, frat rats and dorm dorks that he remembered, and instead, sitting around the round oak tables, he found himself confronted with a motley bunch of hippies, would be radicals, and an occasional professor...all in deep discussions while listening to the loud music that reverberated throughout the hall, bouncing off the domed ceilings, and adding to the flavor of the place...a flavor he wasn't sure he wanted to taste. Some look up when he walked in, but soon went back to their conversations. To his right the eternal bridge players were sitting at a table they had reserved for themselves. It was rumored that they had been playing bridge there daily since the early 50's. They were about the only familiar faces he remembered from his short semester at the University, not so long ago in time, but already lost in his personal history.

Walking past them, he ordered coffee and two cheese and egg sandwiches at the Rat's cafeteria; paid, and picked up his tray scanning the crowded room looking for an available place to sit and have breakfast. Someone called his name and looking around noticed Dennis' upraised hand motioning him to come over.

"So you got my note?" Dennis asked.

"Yeah. Stella was gone." he shrugged.

"Stella is a free soul, she comes, and goes when she wants, sleeps with whoever strikes her fancy, and she never looks back."

He sighed, "Yeah...just want I needed."

"Look you got a Mercy Fuck, so don't knock it." Dennis shrugged.

Changing the subject seemed like a good idea, "You look a bit nervous. What's bothering you Dennis?"

"I dropped acid last night and again this morning. I'm somewhat paranoid and freaked out. I think there are Narcs in the Rat." His eyes followed a hugely obese woman who was circling their table like a hungry shark.

"Do you know her Dennis?"

"God yes. Her name is Robin and normally she plays bridge with that bunch over there." Dennis indicated the bridge players table. "But she won't play now since she thinks she's been cursed. She also believes that I might know someone who can help her."

"So, give her something and let her get on with her life."

Dennis didn't seem to hear, and just went on talking. "She thinks she has her own private ghost too, or at least she says so. Nobody's ever seen it except her, of course, but she insists that it's friendly and very male...oh God no—she's going to join us!"

"So you can introduce us," he teased.

Dennis tensed up and sort of hunkered down for the worse, much like a tortes retreating into its shell, but then Robin changed direction and sat down with one of the skinniest people in the Rat. "Wait...good, good. Thank God; she's gone after Walden."

Walden?" he raised an eyebrow.

"Yeah that skinny Mexican kid she just sat with goes by the name "Walden" like the poet. He's been fucking her for months." Dennis paused to let the notion sink in. "Can you imagine *anyone* screwing that hulk? How and the hell does he manage to spread her legs wide enough. Well, he IS really skinny." Dennis added as an afterthought.

It was time to change the subject again, "so what are you writing about?" Dennis was always either writing or painting and he excelled at both.

"It's ad-lib poetry. Walden and I used to sit here and write it to one another. It's about the people you see in here, and some you think you'd never like to see again. This is the same sort of thing that Gladys used to do when she came here; listening to what people say, copying their conversations, and putting them into poems. I call it eaves dropping in verse. This one here is about an old lady that grows pot in her kitchen."

Gladys was a close friend of his mother. She had been the librarian at Dunkirk for years and now worked in the University Agricultural Library on the other side of the sprawling campus and she considered herself one of the avant-garde. Her poems were witty if a bit spiteful and as she would say they contained many hidden "double entendres"; a word that she pronounced in what she believe to be a French accent.

"Old Walden is a homophile." Dennis said, and then looked at him questioningly.

"Ok, what's a homophile?"

"You Marines would call him a fag, or a queer."

"I thought you said he was fucking fats over there."

"Oh yeah, that's right, so it makes him Bi. He's a speed freak anyway, so anything's possible with Walden."

Dennis got up abruptly, went to the cafeteria, and came back with two more cups of steaming coffee. They fell silent; Dennis went back to his writing, while he stared, somewhat vacantly, at the unfamiliar faces surrounding them and thought, 'so this is the world that we fought for; a changed world, without any of the old values.' He looked around at all the people who benefited by their 2-S college deferments; oblivious to the life and death struggle going on in Vietnam, only interested in condemning any young American foolish enough to be involved in it. Everyone was turning on, drinking coffee, and enjoying the leisure to condemn and criticize at the cost of some eighteen-year-old who wasn't fortunate enough to get a deferment—partying and laughing while unnoticed, eighteen-year-old blood soaked into the mud and dust of Vietnam, becoming one with Asia. The question that came to his mind was "why"? Had he learned anything from his time in Vietnam? And, who were these strangers sitting at the oak tables? He had fought in a few square miles of hell, just as the VC and NVA fought; neither side concerned with much more than staying alive. So what had he brought back from Asia? Nothing more than some temporarily dormant malaria and a rock-hard conviction that there would be no future, or at least, no future of which he could ever be a part. Thinking about it, he just wanted to call the whole thing off—to turn the clock back or maybe stop time and find a way to live in a world that only had black and white realities based on living or dying. A world without all the killing—but, he couldn't, there were no such worlds, and even if they existed someplace, there wasn't anything he could do about it—because to him, nothing mattered any longer.

As he pressed his forehead, trying to force his mind to stop thinking, he could almost visualize black walls closing in on him from all sides sealing him from the reality of those fortunate, happy favored people sitting at their round oaken tables and thinking that they could change the world; never knowing or caring that the world was a beast of prey waiting to devour them if the war lasted longer than their 2-S deferments

Two girls walked in and Dennis waved them over. Dennis whispered, "The one in front is Rose, and the other is her sister, Miki."

"Hi Dennis!" Rose said as she sat down. She wore her hair very short and her bell-bottom Jeans tight. Her sister, Miki, wore alarmingly short mini, nylons and had long silky black hair that cascaded far below her shoulders.

"Hi," Dennis said, "so what's happening?"

Miki made a face, "A real tragedy. They busted our supplier last week, and nearly got my brother too."

Dennis, ever paranoid, placed a finger on his lips.

"Oh really, Dennis"! Rose said, "Like, you think everyone is a Narc." He felt her eyes search his face, "Ok maybe your friend here looks like a Narc, but it would be too obvious. What is he anyway?"

"He's in the Marines," Dennis offered, "and just got back from Vietnam."

Her eyes widened a little and she exchanged looks with Miki. "Oh, really? A real marine? So what's it like over there, I mean, killing all those women and children...and babies."

Dennis cut in before he could answer, "Tim, there was a demonstration after you left school against Dow Chemical for manufacturing Napalm. Their recruiters came to the campus and this place exploded. It was about a year ago last October, and things got ugly and violent. The anti-war people and a few hundred students took over the Commerce building. The Pigs attacked the demonstrators, broke windows, and hauled students out through the broken glass. Man, even the frat rats were so pissed they attacked the cops."

"I was there," Rose said, "I got this." She showed him a long white scar on her arm, "I was bleeding all over from the broken glass...fifteen stitches, and after the University medic patched me up they arrested him."

"We wanted to stop people like you from burning the Vietnamese children alive." Miki said.

"You mean making us stop from making more Crispy Critters?" he had enough from them and knew he was losing it, but couldn't help himself.

Her eyebrows shot up, "What does a breakfast cereal shaped like animals have to do with war crimes?"

He paused, lit a cigarette, and sat back in his chair. "We call them Crispy Critters...you know, the burnt remains after our napalm fries them."

She choked and he thought she might throw up, "How could you."

"Well, it's pretty simple. When you're holding on by the skin of your teeth, and outnumbered by maybe four to one, you call in those Phantoms and they drop the stuff on the enemy. If some kids get wasted—well sorry 'bout that shit, little dink grow into big Cong. The NVA don't have Napalm so they use white phosphorous airbursts on us. You know what White Phosphorous can do? No, you don't, do you. It hits your skin and burns and sinks in, and continues to burn using the oxygen from your blood to keep it smoldering until it comes out the other side, or someone takes a knife and cuts off a big chunk of your flesh with the dam stuff still burning and gets it off you. Did you protest the North Vietnamese use of white phosphorous on us when you protested against napalm?"

He didn't expect an answer. The girls just looked at him with hate and disgust and Dennis was sitting very quietly; he could tell Dennis wanted to be anywhere but at the table.

The other tables near them had gone quiet as well. "So..." she said, "I take it you are for the war."

He closed his eyes for a minute. "Your name is Rose, right?" he said.

"And they call you Miki?" the girls nodded. "So it's like this. No one who has ever fought in any war is in favor of wars. But it doesn't really matter what I think, does it. I'm sure you don't give a damn and I certainly don't." he paused looking for the words, trying to reach out and make her see what he was, what they all were...the ones fighting over there on the other side of the world. He wanted them to understand the way he felt. "War is insanity. Stupid waste filled with bullshit moralization on both sides, but in the end, it is just a bunch of grim dirty tired grunts that fight and die because there really isn't much of a choice over there, where all the lies and falsehoods are meaningless; the only thing that matters is living and keeping your buddies alive, nothing else matters."

"You killed babies." Rose said. He knew she would never understand. This girl, becoming a woman in the aquarium of the University, was brimming over with idealism, searching for a cause, to hold her interest—between boyfriends and parties.

As the memories struck him like a tidal wave, a tear formed in his eye, "Yes, we killed babies. But never intentionally, or at least I don't think we did."

She looked at him and then pronounced, "We don't like you. And they don't like you." She indicated the people sitting around them. "None of us like you—we don't want you here. You don't belong."

He looked around at the hostile faces in the adjoining tables. "Yeah. Thanks a lot. God bless America." he got up and started to walk to the door.

"Power to the people, killer!" Someone shouted. He paused, and then turned, and while he felt like throwing a punch, he couldn't bring himself strike out at the people he had promised to protect. He just stared at them for a while. Some looked down and seemed embarrassed, while others smiled and raised their arm in the communist salute, making a fist, then turning it and extending their middle finger. He turned his back on everything, and walked out of the Union. The music swallowed them, getting softer and weaker as he left the hall, finally washing everything away as he felt the total futility of it all—and he clung to his mantra: 'nothing matters'.

Dennis followed him outside. "I'm sorry about what happened, Tim," he said, "but you have to understand, things are changing. Just keep cool, and when you get out and go back to school, grow some hair, and pretend you never went into the Marines and never spent a day in Vietnam."

They sat together by the fountain just outside of the Student Union and watched several drug deals in progress. "Those people in there, sitting, talking, drinking coffee...they're strangers to me, and when I think about coming back here, if I live through the next year, I can't really be a part of this brave new world. When I left school things were a lot different; now it's just another battleground like Vietnam, only worse because here the people who hate you are your own countrymen. Even with long hair and pretending I never did what I did and became what I am—I won't fit in." he paused, took a drag on the joint Dennis handed him. "Fuck it. I have to report in to the Marine Reserve Unit down on Wright Street."

"Before you go just remember something." Dennis said as they passed the joint. "Don't be too hard on them. They're young and none of them have actually met the real people you have, the people that bled and died with you...we can only imagine what it was like, but I see it in your eyes—the pain. You seem so old now—so tired. You knew what you were doing back there, didn't you. You wanted to freak them out."

He thought about it and then answered. "Yes, I suppose I did. But which is better? Letting them go on in their ignorance, or showing the truth."

"Whose truth?" Dennis said. "Yours? Mine? The government? I think that the only truth worth having is to live, to write, paint, listen to great music, and concentrate on the things that don't change. Look around you, Tim. This isn't real. It's only the 'now'."

"Well," he smiled, "my "now" is getting my ass over to the Reserve Center and reporting in. After that I can think about tomorrow."

It was a short drive down Washington Ave. to the Marine Corps reserve building, which was located just off East Johnson Street. As soon as he entered the building he knew it was the Marine Corps... everything was spick and span, and squared away. There wasn't much activity, so he knocked on the door of the first office he saw.

"Enter"

Opening the door, he saw a Master Gunnery Sergeant, his breast covered with ribbons. The Gunny looked up and indicated a chair, "Sit down, how can I help you?"

"I'm Brad...sorry Corporal T.C. Bratvold, Gunny, and I came home on emergency leave, and was told to check in." he slid a copy of his traveling orders to the Gunny who picked them up and quickly read the paper. Putting the orders back on the table, he looked at him for a full minute then said, "I'm sorry about your mother...Brad. I know this isn't what you expected to come home to."

"Thank you Gunny."

"Normally your leave would be over in another ten days; you would report back, get your travel documents, airline tickets, and be off to the West Coast for shipping out to Vietnam," he hesitated, "but there seems to be some discussion in Marine Corps HQ whether or not to send you back at all. I had a phone call about you and for now just take those ten days—it's never easy losing someone close and you look like you could use a little down time; then report back here to the reserve center where you will be temporarily detached to us for duty until your final orders arrive. Not much going on right now, so essentially you'll be working with me getting the training program set up for our reservists."

"Is that all Gunny?" he asked.

"For now. When you get back the old man will probably want to talk to you." and, as he started to turn, the Gunny added, "Brad—things have changed since you've been away. Don't let it get to you. The way they— well, it isn't like WWII or Korea."

"Thanks Gunny. I'll see you next week then."

"We'll get you squared away with some utilities, and get you whatever you are missing in terms of a uniform. Your stuff is probably back with your unit in Vietnam or in storage some place on Okinawa. Don't worry; I'll get you squared away when you get back." They shook hands and he thanked the gunny then left the building. It was strange that now, for the first time since he arrived back in the states, he felt truly at home...the Marines hadn't changed, maybe the entire world had gone to hell, but the Marines seemed unchanged, and it made him feel better.

On the return drive, he kept replaying what happened in the Rat over and over again. Finally, he turned on the radio and tried to forget everything but the happier times. He remembered the trips to the Mississippi River where he had spent days duck hunting with his uncle. They had stayed in a friend's small house trailer that was permanently parked on Battle Island, and as he drove, he wanted to get away from Dunkirk, and return to that crisp clean land of his memories.

Returning home, he called Joe, the owner, and after they exchanged the obligatory greetings, and Joe had expressed his sorrow over the death, they agreed that he could use the house trailer until the weekend. His next call was to Dennis to see if he wanted to come along. Dennis picked up the phone, and said he just got back from Madison himself, and said again how sorry he was for what had happened in the Rat. He listened to the proposed trip and readily agreed to join the adventure.

Dennis passed the phone to someone. "Tim?" she said. It was Stella. "You and Dennis weren't thinking about going on a trip without me were you?" she teased.

"No, of course not." he lied. "Be ready early tomorrow. Ok?"

"With bells on." She said enthusiastically.

Wally had overheard the conversation and asked him to join him for a cup of coffee. As they sat in the Netterblad's spotless kitchen and sipped the strong black brew, he could tell Wally wanted to say something, and several times the man almost started, then hesitated, looked at his hands until, finally taking the initiative, he broke Wally's silence said, "I plan to take off tomorrow and spend a few days on the Mississippi River. I thought it might be easier if I just go back to my grandmothers after the trip. I appreciate everything, Wally, really I do, but I get the feeling that I'm imposing on you."

"It's not that, Tim. We want you here, but you are so changed. You almost never come down from your room during the day, not even to eat, and we hear you coming back late," he began, "I know you're not the same boy we used to know, and I know it isn't my business, but we think your Mother would have wanted you to behave differently."

He didn't want to hurt Wally, so only said, "I have things to work out."

"Did they have any news at the Reserve Center?"

Grateful for a change in the conversation he said, "Yeah. They might not send me back. I have a little time to recover and then will be starting work at the Reserve center next Monday until my orders come through."

Wally smiled, "That's great news! I pulled all the strings I could to get them to consider letting you stay in the States. You've done enough...and your all there is left of her."

Not knowing what to say, he said nothing.

"Your mother made a terrible mistake when she married that man. She started drinking, and I never knew her to take more than a glass of wine at Christmas until he came back into her life. One day she came to work bruised and I think Leo beat her...he was a mean drunk you know. She was loyal...so loyal...never said he did it, but then she told me she had started drinking with Leo, to keep him company so he wouldn't go out to the taverns, she claimed. She probably found out that he was cheating on her as well. He cheated so openly everyone knew about it. The neighbors said there a lot of empty bottles in their trash, and she locked herself away from everyone...wouldn't take any help. No, Lenore wouldn't let anyone help her...she was so proud—too proud. I stood up for them at the wedding; at least Leo had enough decency to make their arrangement legal. God, oh God." Wally was in tears, "She was such a wonderful girl—my girl—my secretary—my Lenore —and he dragged her down, down, down..."

"Do you still think Leo killed her?" he asked.

"I know he did—and if I can put him away, I will." Wally wiped his eyes. "Anyway, the trip will be good for you. Don't make any decisions about moving out. Start work at the Reserve Center and let's see where it goes from there."

"Sure thing." he said, not knowing what else to say. "I'll be leaving early tomorrow morning for the River." It amazed him how quickly people could go from talking about death to trivial matters. To him death was a reality—the only reality—and life only seemed like a short interlude.

He went up to his room...John's room, collapsed in the soft bed, thinking he would take a short nap, close his eyes, and try not to think about anything.

• • •

It had been raining forever. They joked about never seeing the sun again, but Ski always helped them forget the mud and rain of the monsoon. Ski was a part of the "Old Corps," hard drinking, loyal to a fault, and never afraid. When they would return to the base camp Ski was always there waiting for them, with a bottle of Jack Daniels and a warm stove in the quartermaster's tent where they would sit around that glowing potbellied oil heater, pass the bottle, and listen to him regal them with stories of Guam, Iwo, Guadalcanal and the "Frozen Chozen," that terrible march to the sea when the 1st Marines were fighting uncounted Chinese divisions for their lives and for the honor of the Corps.

"Hell this war ain't shit." he lifted a leg and farted loudly into the stove. They laughed and accused Ski of trying to gas them. Then Ski stopped and just stared at the rain pouring down outside of the tent, his face as sad as any he had ever seen, then, pulling himself together with a 'what the hell' shrug he went back to his story telling until someone came in and gave him a letter from home. Ski just sat there, holding it in his hand unopened.

"Didn't know you knew anyone could read" someone kidded him.

Ski smiled weakly, and said. "Well, my wife reads and even knows how to write," he chuckled, "and anyway, since it's from her I better open it up." Ski read the letter, closed his eyes, and then read it again. They watched his eyes flow over the words.

"Something wrong Ski?" he asked.

"Naw...nothing, nothing Brad. There's just one swig left in this bottle. Finish it...my gift to you, boy."

Then ski got up and just walked out into the rain, the letter still clutched in his hand. His fire-team looked at each other for a minute and started to get up. Before they could follow him outside the sound of a shot stopped them cold, and then they all ran out of the tent where they found Ski, face down in the mud, the rain, and blood making a

115

crimson puddle around what was left of his head. The letter had fallen out of his hand, and now it was stained with mud, blood, and Vietnam. They never looked at the letter, just picked Ski up, and ground the letter into the mud with their boots...deeper and deeper into that goddamned mud as they lifted old Ski—damn letter—damn rain—damn everything. They took Ski back to the tent, rolled him up in a poncho, and then loaded him into the back of the Captains jeep. No one said anything then...or ever.

CHAPTER 8

The early morning sun woke him; he rubbed the sleep from his eyes. He had been crying in his sleep again. With a sigh, he got up, showered, shaved, and packed for the trip.

He pulled to the curb in front of Dennis' apartment and honked. The first one down to the car was Stella. "Shotgun!" she called, and then sort of hesitated, and then looked down and said, "Sorry. I didn't mean..."

"Yeah, ok. Shotgun it is," he answered, and then added, "and what about Dennis?"

"Oh," she said, "You know Dennis. He had to get his brushes, paints and whatnots together and will be down in a few minutes."

It was getting cooler as the month approached November, and he had the car heater on. They sat in the front seat waiting for Dennis.

"Are you and Dennis...?" he asked.

She laughed. "No, but not for lack of trying. He's a friend, and a lot of fun, but even though a lot of us have tried, as far as I know he never got involved with a girl."

"Is he...?"

"Dennis is Dennis," she said firmly, "and what he is or isn't—that's his own business, does it matter to you?"

He thought about it for a few moments and then said, "No. No it doesn't. As you said, he's a friend."

Dennis joined them, and they dropped the subject. It was a long way to the river, and he took the back roads, so well-known to him from earlier happier times, when every October he would spend some time at the River. He had always been a loner in High School, vastly preferring to hunt and fish in the wild to competing in varsity sports, which he had found both uninteresting and repetitive.

With everything stored, and the little VW gassed up and ready, they pulled out of Dunkirk, heading North on Highway 51, then taking a country road toward Oregon, with the intention of rendezvousing with Highway 151, then Westward passing the mythical haunted Ridgeway Valley, and on toward the magical father of waters; the Mississippi.

The miles and hours passed slowly, and they would pull over to admire the landscape and the amazing architecture incongruously nestled in the small forgotten towns of Western Wisconsin.

"Look at that house!" Dennis exclaimed. He was excited. "Wait! Wait! Pull over just for a second!"

They pulled over for what seemed to him to be the hundredth time. The house was truly beautiful in its symmetry. Field stone porches, solid brick up to gabled the windows and their sharp sloping roofs. Two towers adorned the left and right sides of the house, with a pointed third floor roof and each one had windows that allowed for a 360-degree view. The windows over the main entrance and in the two towers had stained glass half-panes with Art Nouveau motifs.

"Oh god, look at that architecture...the stained glass windows...look the windows are Art Nouveau![12]" Dennis would spend hours painstakingly painting in the Art Nouveau style, and also recreating stained glass designs for clients. His current hero was Louis Comfort Tiffany, the creator of the famous Tiffany lamps and other designs. For the next half hour, he regaled them with stories about art and Tiffany lamps.

As they continued driving toward the river, the old houses became more frequent, but Dennis had fallen asleep in the back seat, so they didn't wake him and finally started making better time on the journey. Dennis was right, he thought, these were more than just houses, they were homes, and represented a life that had already become obsolete, yet—they cloistered the memories of their long lives in the empty rooms, the shadowed gables, and behind the climbing ivy now turning brown and red as winter approached.

The houses reminded him of his honorary grandfather and Christmas Eve, when everyone sat around the tree in the living room,

---

[12] Art Nouveau was a movement in the visual arts popular from the early 1890s up to the First World War.

and the tavern was closed for Christmas so no noise came from downstairs to intrude on the peace, as his surrogate grandfather, his mother's Uncle Ben, would signal that it was time to open the presents. No one ever had the patience to wait until morning. He remembered the smell of the tree and Christmas cookies fresh from the oven, Uncle Ben, Aunt Dora, his mother and him. And then, when he was in Vietnam, they all died. First Ben and Dora and then his mother. Seeming to sense his pain, Stella put her hand on his knee and as she placed her head on his shoulder he took her hand, held it letting the memories pass. Christmas was over forever.

She was still dozing on his shoulder as he came to a large bluff overlooking the Mississippi. He stopped the car and soaked in the vision of "Old Man River" rolling majestically to the sea. This was a mystical magical land of bluffs and sky, tree covered hillsides rolling down into the valleys, their small towns, usually no more than a few hundred people at most, safe and solid against rain, wind and clouds. He could almost hear Mark Twain talking about this restless river, with the constantly changing land that formed its boundaries both East and West. He felt a kinship here and also a welcoming. Yet with that welcoming was the feeling that this would not be the end of anything, but just another new beginning. More than anything else, this land was *his*...solid in his memories, bought and paid for in his pain, and he would fight to keep it that way.

He glanced in the mirror at Dennis sleeping soundly, and gently kissed Stella's head. His friends would never see it in the same way as he had every time he came here—came home. This was his secret place, he would only share the entire complexity of it with someone very special, he knew that this would be the last time he'd be here, on the bluff over his beloved river, and that he would never see it again. So he was a drowning man, taking his last lungful of air, which must be savored and stored with everything he was seeing now...burned into his memory. Soon they would stop at the general store in the five-house village of Victory, and he'd drink ice-cold water from the artesian well that flowed from the rocks in the bluff, and then down through a culvert to the river that ran wild and untamed in freedom to the sea.

A DESTINY OF MEMORIES

In the past, this great river ran backwards from South to North for a short period of time. He was amazed to come upon a story which recorded that one of the most powerful quakes to hit North America occurred in the Midwest had caused this and coincidentally fulfilled a prophecy by Tecumseh, the chief of the last great Native American alliance against the ever encroaching whites. He had warned reluctant warrior-tribes that he would stamp his feet and bring down their houses. Sure enough, between December 16, 1811, and late April 1812, a catastrophic series of earthquakes shook the Mississippi and the river ran backwards. While the interpretation of this event varied from tribe to tribe, one consensus was universally accepted: the powerful earthquake had to have meant something. For many tribes it meant that Tecumseh, war chief and the Prophet in the last coalition against the whites must be supported.

Before leaving for Vietnam, he had taken Linda to see his river. They had stopped in this exact place. The memory of her hit him with almost tangible force and his head ached as she invaded his thoughts.

• • •

They had left the car, and she stood in front of him, soaking in the view and the warmth of the sun as it made the river sparkle. He stood behind her, his arms circling her waist and he was in love, she would wait for him, and he would fight a war for his beloved country, return and they would start a life together.

• • •

They had promised each other the foolish promises of youth, but now he was an old man, newly returned alive from the war and she was gone, and there was nothing here except the river. But the River still welcomed him.

• • •

120

There was a Catholic church down the road. She insisted they stop there, and she lit a candle for his safety, but something had changed in her, and when they left that old deserted church, he knew that he would lose her.

· · ·

He looked at Stella and at Dennis, and for a moment, he had a feeling that maybe he could begin again. He woke them and they all stood on that same bluff looking at the river, his hand in hers and her in Dennis'.

"There's something we should look at down the road," he said.

"What's that?" Dennis asked.

"A great old church with stained glass windows and weathered siding."

"Sounds great."

Stella smiled at him and nodded her head in agreement.

It was a short ride to the church, and, as usual, the door was open. They went inside and admired the windows. He paused, and then lit a candle.

"I didn't know you're Catholic." Dennis said. He was old school catholic and lit a candle as well.

"No. I don't know what I am, but I was just lighting it for someone."

Dennis started to say something but Stella shook her head, and he just nodded. She put her arm around him and whispered, "For your mother?"

He didn't answer. "It's ok." She said, and also lit a candle.

There was a small restaurant near the Church, and they stopped in for a quick supper before continuing down river to the Island. They ate hamburgers and watched the sunlight slowly disappear into the shadows cast by the bluff as evening replaced day, and the chariot of the sun moved relentlessly westward. And then, the dark purple sky was replaced by black velvet filled with stars. It would still be some time before moonrise, and he relished the Wisconsin night, so devoid of the fear and the noises of Vietnam.

He wanted to say something to them about the relief he felt that this, at least, had not changed but he kept silent until they were in the car and starting the final leg to the house trailer waiting for them on Battle Island. He wanted to tell them about a picture that he had brought home before shipping out. His mother framed it and hung it in his room. "I had a picture of the guys I shipped out with, hanging in my room. It was an old fashioned group picture about 18 inches long; we were 120 strong when we shipped out." He couldn't go on. He didn't want to know how many died, or how many were crippled in body or in mind. He just didn't want to know.

"And?" Stella prompted him.

"And nothing." he said. "There was just this picture hanging in my room. When I came home I couldn't find it."

"I saw it." Dennis said. "I saw it a little while after you left. She was typing my book for me. You had that great electric Smith Corona in your room and until she moved out to the other place, she would type there. She said it made her feel closer to you."

"It wasn't there at the new house, just the Smith Corona, but no picture on the wall."

Dennis seemed genuinely concerned, "I hope it wasn't lost when they moved."

"It's only a picture."

"Yes, a picture, but it meant something to her. You were there in the first row."

He didn't know whether Dennis was humoring him or not. They turned off the blacktop and were moving through a culvert, which led to a dirt road crossing a rickety bridge linking Battle Island with the mainland. Much of the area was swamp, but on the higher ground was a state park, now closed for the winter, and a cluster of summer shanties and house trailers that were used by the "Summer People", but now empty and lifeless, their windows reflecting neither light nor warmth.

The trailer was near the waterline, on a raised plot of ground, just high enough to keep it safe from flooding but close enough to enjoy an unencumbered view of the river. From upriver, a long line of barges were being towed; a search light flickered back and forth along the channel as the river pilot looked for signs of sunken objects. The search light was in eerie contrast to the soft illumination of the rising moon whose reflection already danced on the waters. The river was expecting him. He unlocked the door, and turned on the lights. "Looks like everything is still hooked up." He turned on a small space heater to take the chill off. The trailer was clean, fully equipped, with a bedroom and a small couch, which opened into a bed.

"There's an outhouse around the back, and a hot water shower next to it." He explained.

Stella took his and her backpack and put it in the bedroom. "We sleep here." She declared. "Dennis, you get the fold-out." Then she efficiently went into the little kitchen, held the cups up for inspection, shook her head in disapproval, then rewashed them and put the coffee pot on the small burner to boil. He and Dennis exchanged bemused smiles, and sat down at the small table next to the kitchenette, which was now, obviously her domain.

He could see she loved Dennis in a special way and that was fine as long as she made love to him. It was as if she was joining the missing parts of her life into one when the three of them were together. He listened to them talking about art, music, and Eastern Religion. She served the coffee and sat between them, her hand kneading his thigh as she and Dennis talked into the night. He didn't have anything to contribute and doubted that they would listen if he had, since they were totally absorbed in each other, and it was only her demanding hand that kept him seated and let him know that he was on her mind.

Finally, she stretched and said, "I'm for bed." They helped Dennis get settled in the foldout bed and then she led him by the hand into the bedroom. Just before she closed the door, she looked back, smiled coquettishly at Dennis, and said, "Sleep tight."

They undressed and made love. As she snuggled into his enfolding arm she pressed her face against his chest and kissed him, "You know that I don't love you. I love Dennis, but he can't—you know, so sometimes I pretend you're him."

"I know," he said, "and I don't love you either."

She sighed contentedly. "Good. I don't want you hurt."

As she fell into an exhausted slumber, he softly stroked her, looked at the ceiling and enjoyed the feeling of her warmth pressing against him. His mind was filled with a SF book by Heinlein called *"Stranger in a strange land"* that had a situation similar to his. That year there was a song called "Triad"...he remembered that the lyrics had used a sentence from Heinlein; *Sister Lovers, water brothers, and in time maybe others.* This was the "now"; he was in bed with a warm attractive girl, and it didn't matter if she didn't love him, because he didn't know if he would ever let himself love again. He would give her what she wanted and take what he needed. He sighed and felt his entire body relax. He smiled ironically to himself, *'from each according to his abilities and to each according to his needs'* he thought.

He told himself to think of it as R & R, like Bangkok or any other place where you went to get laid, drunk or stoned, and enjoy things like cold drinks and flush toilets...his America was gone but what was left of it was pleasant enough if taken out of context. He kissed her forehead and thought she said something in her sleep. The important thing for him wasn't whether she cared or not, it was that he was warm, and safe. No one was trying to kill him, and he wasn't in Dunkirk where the memory of what once was contrasted so horribly with the now. He thought about praying, but other than praying to stay alive, which was no long necessary, he couldn't think of anything else to say—or ask for. He was home. He was alive and no matter what would happen next, he was starting to feel happy. His last conscious thought as he felt himself drifting off was *'Hope I don't dream',* and then, like a mantra, he whispered that thought to the night, hoping it would close that floodgate of memories and dreams.

●   ●   ●

The dawn, of course, never comes up like thunder in real life, rather it sneaks up on you, stepping quietly like a jungle cat, until it has you firmly in its paws, and if you lay perfectly still, sometimes, just sometimes, even here in America you could still hear the Grateful Dead as they pulled the chariot of the sun, back from Vietnam, bringing the light of another day to Wisconsin and to the River. He lay silently for a while, enjoying Stella, then not wishing to disturb her, he slipped out of the bed, and taking his clothes into the other room, quietly dressed.

He crept past a gently snoring Dennis, opened the door, and stepped outside into the bracing chill of the morning. He walked passed the shuttered shacks and empty camping trailers, following the dusty road that led to the picnic area, now covered in a deep layer of dead leaves. The dead leaves curled around his legs and it almost felt like he was wading through a multi-colored sea. The only sound was the crackling paper-like song of the still dead leaves being startled into temporary life by his passing. He found an old picnic table and sat on the tabletop, using the bench to support his booted feet.

Lighting a cigarette he took a deep breath, inhaling the tobacco mixed with the cool river air, as he tried to bring back visions of other times when he had spent weekends at that exact spot, enjoying the rough comradery of his hunting buddies. Looking up, he let his eyes follow the tree line of the towering bluffs until on the very highest point, and there in a treeless area, he saw what had once been huge cross that had been made from two logs. The last time he had visited the river with Linda they had climbed the bluff to take a closer look at the cross. It was a dead log, which had been set in a hole, with another log nailed and tied in place. They had searched for a grave or some other reason for this lonely marker, but found nothing but this tree trunk symbolically reaching into the sky, as if it were seeking some sort of redemption. Linda had said that she thought the cross was waiting for something to happen. He had felt a chill then and thought '*or for someone to die*' and they never looked back. The rope had finally rotted through since then, and now, instead of a cross, it was a lopsided X.

He heard a rustling in the leaves and looked up to see Dennis walking toward him. He nodded good morning as Dennis took a seat on the tabletop. Dennis sat in silence for a while then said, "It isn't working is it."

"What do you mean, Dennis?"

"You know...I mean you're not really here are you."

He thought about it and said. "It's better now, but I'm still missing something."

Dennis sighed. "So, let's go back to the trailer, and have breakfast."

A DESTINY OF MEMORIES

When they returned to the trailer, Stella was already awake scrambling some eggs in the black cast iron skillet utilizing the left over grease of freshly fried bacon. The aroma of fresh percolated coffee filled the trailer and he was starved.

Later, he took them downriver to see the incredible home of H. Louis Dousman, a fur trader, and a lumberman who made his fortune in the 1840's. It was called the Villa Louis and had been a place that he revisited every time that he came home to his river. He was searching for memories; those elusive wisps of half remembered mist, concealing much, but revealing tantalizing glimpses of the sights and sounds that could comfort him, dancing in his mind like a stripper, showing him just enough to keep him coming back for more.

They spent the day walking through the Villa, which was now a museum, and exploring the old graveyards in the small villages. Each headstone told a story, some of the Blackhawk Wars, others of both loss, and grief. The little towns, with names like Victory and Defeat, stood as silent testament to that short and bloody war which had seen the end of Chief Black Hawk's attempt to keep a foothold in his ancestral lands east of the Mississippi.

Black Hawk was reported as saying this in his *"Autobiography of Ma-Ka-Tai-Me-She-Kia or Black Hawk by Black Hawk"*: When you return to your chief, I want you to tell him all my words. Tell him that Black Hawk's eyes have looked upon many suns, but they shall not see many more; and that his back is no longer straight, as in his youth, but is beginning to bend with age. The Great Spirit has whispered among the treetops in the morning and evening and says that Black Hawk's days are few, and that he is wanted in the spirit land. He is half-dead, his arm shakes and is no longer strong, and his feet are slow on the warpath. Tell him all this, and tell him, too, that Black Hawk would have been a friend to the whites, but they would not let him, and that the hatchet was dug up by themselves and not by the Indians. Tell your chief that Black Hawk meant no harm to the pale faces when he came across the Mississippi, but came peaceably to raise corn for his starving women and children, and that even then he would have gone back, but when he sent his white flag the braves who carried it were treated like squaws and one of them inhumanly shot. Tell him too, that Black Hawk will have revenge, and that he will never stop until the Great Spirit shall say to him, 'come away.'

Over the next two days, they explored more of the surrounding hill country, again, stopping at ancient graveyards where Dennis would make rubbings from the tombstones, the names, and dates of long gone people, taking shape in his sketches. Then before he realized it, it was time to leave this haven and return. They cleaned the trailer, leaving it exactly as they found it, packed the VW, and started for home. Leaving the valley they traveled East on highway 151, passed the secretive Ridgway valley, and turned off on a shortcut which took them to Highway 51 and the final road to home. Stella dozed on his shoulder and Dennis, as usual, snored quietly in the back seat. Stella had become important to him, he could still feel her need, and even if it wasn't for him, he was grateful for the time they had spent together. It could have been anyone, sitting next to him in the car, giving him some reason to keep on trying, and he'd feel the same way; grateful for a distraction from death and war. He needed something real to hang on to, and Stella had been there for him; real and warm, and far more complicated than anyone he had ever loved. Did he love her? He realized it didn't matter if she was using him; he wanted her and her blind raw passion, which overwhelmed his sadness and detachment. Whatever she could offer he would accept gratefully because he realized that at least for this short period of time, she was his salvation. He would love this green-eyed girl and not just for the few days they had spent together. He would love her because she eased his pain when there was nothing left for him. And if he was a substitute for Dennis, so be it. She had held his pain and memories at bay, sheltering him with her body. He knew that this trip had been a way to say goodbye to each other, and the real lesson she had taught him was that life and love are the same thing and that he had to try again and again or something would die inside. The wound would heal and scars would form...but the scars would be his badge of courage.

It was early evening by the time he pulled up in front of Dennis' apartment. He helped them unload and they said their goodbye's there at the curb. As they started up the outside stairs, which lead to the apartment Stella paused for a moment, looked back, and gave him a sad smile and a small wave. He didn't want to return to the Netterblad's house until he made a last visit to his mother's home.

He wasn't sure that Pam would still be there since she was expecting to move in with her Aunt in Madison until things worked out with her father. As he pulled up to the house in the gathering dusk of Wisconsin in late October, he saw that there was a light on in the living room and also on the porch. He parked and walked to the door, hesitated, wondering if he should knock or not, then, realizing that this was not his home and never would be, he hesitantly tapped lightly on the frosted glass window.

Pam opened the door. "Hi stranger." She said. She asked him to sit down on the sofa and brought him a cup of coffee, which she placed next to her own half empty cup, adjacent to an ashtray overflowing with cigarette butts.

"So where have you been?" she asked.

He sipped his coffee. "I needed to get away from this town for a while."

"Don't I know it!" she said and sighed, "Tim, are you angry with me?"

"No, of course not. Why should I be?"

"It's just that, well, about everything and about what happened before you left, at the party." She locked eyes with him, and then looked down at her hands.

"We all make choices, Pam," he said.

"Choices!" she snapped, "I woke up and this—bastard was standing over me and saying hi, we just made love. And then he sipped up his pants and walked away."

"It's no big thing, Pam. You were drunk and he took advantage. Chalk it up to experience. We all learn the hard way." He knew he was being unnecessarily hard, but didn't feel in a friendly mood.

"But what if I get pregnant?"

He thought about it and decided not to answer. After a while she added, "I mean—having a kid by that sick bastard." She shuddered.

He continued in his silence, certain that this was neither the time nor the place to answer— if he ever would.

Nonplussed by his silence she continued. "I mean—he would have to be sick, wouldn't he. Like, who could get any pleasure from a thing like that?"

Finally, he answered, "Pam. Things happen. Learn from it and get on with your life."

She just continued to look at her hands. "I feel so degraded."

Finally, he couldn't stay silent any longer. "So what do you want me to do about it?"

She looked up, surprised by his gruff tone. "Kill him, Tim—shoot him." And he could tell she was serious.

He was tired of people who had never taken a life asking him to take one for them. He understood her anger but refused to feed it. "And that would solve things, how?" he said quietly, "a death for a life? Not much of a trade, Pam."

Finally, she calmed down. "I guess you're right." She said. "This is my problem and I'll deal with it alone as I always have."

He wanted to hold her hand and tell her that everyone deserves a second chance. The young man that had raped her would probably be dead by this time next year. He had learned a new word from Dennis and Stella, which might apply, and he had learned what they and his grandmother had been trying to tell him. "Karma will take care of him, Pam."

She smiled. "I see you've been talking to Dennis and Stella."

"And my grandmother." He added.

She changed the subject, "So how *is* Stella?" She asked.

"Stella is—Stella." He smiled.

"She doesn't love you." It wasn't a question, just a quiet statement of fact, "She won't love anyone—she can't."

"I know," he said, "we agreed never to love each other."

"Don't get her pregnant," she added.

"Thanks for the advice but that would be up to her, wouldn't it?" Then somewhat more kindly he added, "she knows what she's doing Pam and I don't she would consider me husband material. I could be dead this time next year."

She was shocked. "But I thought you wouldn't have to go back!"

He thought for a moment and then measured his words, "We never left Vietnam."

"I don't understand you." She said and he could see she was sad.

"None of us will ever leave Vietnam, Pam. We may be here, but maybe the best part of what we were, was left back there in Vietnam. Maybe they will let me stay here in the States for a while to get over what happened here, but in the end, I know I'll go back, because there isn't anything else left for me now."

He saw her sag back into her chair and realized that she knew it was over for them before it even began. "We're not angry with each other, are we Tim?"

"No," he said, "I don't stay angry with friends."

"Ok, friend," she said, "I'm wishing you luck. Go and find what it is you are looking for. The house will be closed and locked but take this extra key, in case you want to say goodbye to it. There were times when we were all happy together here."

He accepted the key, got up and kissed her on the forehead, and left her sitting alone in the big empty living room.

CHAPTER 9

The following Monday at 0800 he reported for duty at the Reserve Center. The Gunny took him to the supply room, handed him a kit bag, and issued him a winter uniform, full set of utilities, boots, socks, and the standard Marine gear. "We work in utilities here, but you should starch and press them. We have to be a good example for the reserves," he said. And then he gave him a clinical once over and pronounced, "First stop is the barber shop down the street." Under the Gunny's direction, the barber gave him a regulation marine haircut.

"There," the Gunny said, "Now you're looking like a Marine NCO again. (Non-Commissioned Officer) It's almost noon, so let's stop over at that bar and grill and have a cheeseburger, fries, and a nice beer." They sat on bar stools and ordered. He reached into his pocket to pay but the Gunny told him that since the reserve offices didn't have a mess hall the noon meal was taken care of. He handed the barkeeper a chit for the two meals.

Back at the reserve center, he changed into his new utilities, squared everything away in the kit bag, and walked into the Gunny's office. "Now that's more like it. The old man wants a word with you and after that we can talk about your duties here. He's in the room down the hall. Just knock and go in. Don't forget we never salute indoors."

"Right Gunny and never salute outdoors either if we are in the 'Nam." he smiled and got a smile in return.

The old man was a lieutenant Colonel of about 50, dressed in his sharp wintergreens, sitting ramrod straight behind the desk. "Sit down Corporal." he said. "During the winter there isn't much going on here, just inventory, and a monthly training weekend. You'll be with us until your paperwork gets straightened out. I expect you to look sharp and help Gunnery Sergeant Hardy with anything he needs. You may be expected to pull a shift or two as overnight NCO, but for the most part, we come to work late and leave early unless something is planned. I understand you have a place to stay?"

"Yes sir." he said.

"Good. Since you will be living off base I'll see to it that you'll be getting off base living expenses while your under my command, I see you have a car so there shouldn't be a problem reporting in every morning on time."

"Right sir."

"Good." Then he softened a bit and added, "I'm sorry for your loss, son. You're a Marine NCO and I know you'll get by it."

"Yes Sir."

"Ok, back to work. If anything comes across my desk, I'll let you know something as soon as I do. Until then, welcome to the outfit." he extended his hand and they shook on it.

That first week was filled with the organized routine of having a duty station; reporting in at 0900, lunch at 1200 and on the way home at 1530. He familiarized himself with the reserve center, talked to the reservists who would stop in from time to time, and assisted the Gunny in maintenance and inventory. He began to learn the rhythm of the life and found that the daily repetition and purpose had a calming effect on him. He tried several times to contact Stella, and stopped by at Dennis' after work, but she had left town and no one knew when or if she would return. "It's Stella." Dennis would say, "Stella's like that. She comes and she goes."

That weekend, when he visited Dennis, she was there. She hugged him and brushed her lips against his. He wanted to ask where she had been but knew better. Stella was a free spirit.

She ran her hand over the stubble of the Marine haircut and laughed, "Look what they did to you."

He smiled and touched his head, "Yeah. Back in the Marines again."

"My poor Tim. Oh well, it'll grow back some day."

He noticed a young man with long straight blond hair reaching down below his collar. "This is John." Stella said, "He's a good friend of Dennis and will be staying with us."

John gave a small wave and greeted him, "Hi Tim. What's happening?"

Not knowing how to answer, he just chose to nod in return. '*So, is this my replacement?*' he thought. Sensing his confusion she offered, "Let's go for a walk."

He nodded in agreement. Then she turned to Dennis and John who were busy discussing some of Dennis' latest work, "Hey guys, I'm going for a walk with Tim. Be back later."

"Peace" John said making the V sign with the two fingers of his right hand.

As they held hands and walked toward the little yellow walking bridge that spanned the Yahara, he kept thinking about how things can change in a short amount of time. The cold November sun shone down on them through denuded trees as they walked in silence. He felt what he had with Stella slipping away. It was something made from nothing and as nothing, it was returning to the dust and the stuff of dreams. It had been a beautiful dream but now, he realized, it was starting to end. Stella had been his lifeline—his anchor, and now it was turning to fog.

They reached the walking bridge and silently stood, resting their arms on the rail, as they look into the dark November waters, still flowing, but soon to be frozen solid in the icy embrace of winter. She didn't say anything and he noticed she was silently crying, the tears marching down her chilled cheeks. "I don't love you, Tim." She said.

"I know. I don't love you either." And he held her close until she stopped crying. They stood like that, huddling together against the chilled wind blowing off the river, and it seemed to him that they must have stayed like that, frozen in time, for an eternity.

Finally, he said, "Is it over for us?"

"You can't trust me, Tim." She said. "You'll be gone soon, either back to Vietnam or to some other faraway place, and you'll be dead to me. I don't want to morn you, it's not my style."

"No promises," he said, "let's live one day at a time. No trust and no love."

"And no jealousy." she said.

During the next two weeks as Thanksgiving approached, they made time for each other as often as they could, walking the tight rope between her life style and his. Every time they met, Stella made the grim realities of what had happened and what he had yet to face, fade as she opened her warmth to him moving deep inside, penetrating the core of his being, entrenching herself there, and becoming a part of him. He knew he was a liar when he said he didn't love her.

Dennis and John moved out to a farmhouse they rented and gave him the keys to the apartment. The lease would be up in 60 days, but until then, he had his own place and making his excuses to the Netterblads, he moved his gear to that upstairs apartment. Stella commuted between the farm and the apartment, he picking her up on his way home from work and dropping her off in the morning on his way back. He never asked her about John and she never volunteer any information but he began to suspect that John wasn't interested in her as a woman.

At the reserve center, his work entered into a solid routine, which lulled him. He would work, pick Stella up, eat supper together, and go to bed. On Saturday, they would visit Dennis and John, smoke pot and listen to music, and then go back to the apartment where they spent the rest of the weekend making love and talking.

"I don't love you." She said again for the umpteenth time.

"I know. I don't love you either."

"I'm a liar too." She smiled.

He smiled back and said, "We're a pair of liars now."

They were next to the window on a mattress, watching the first snow flurries dance their way down to cover the street with a thin frosting of white. "I wish we were going to have more time." he said.

She pressed her finger to his lips. "Don't think about it, Tim."

"Sooner or later I'm going to have to answer the voices."

"Voices?" she asked.

"Sometimes it's a low rumble, like distant thunder, or an artillery barrage far away in the distance, these voices calling me to go back; back to Asia—to Vietnam, to pay what I owe them."

"Don't you dare to go back"! She said, as she rolled over on top of him pressing down covering him with her body as if to protect him. "Don't you dare go back! We can go to Canada and they won't find you there. I have friends...they left before they got drafted. We can stay with them." She was kissing him, forcing him to live, her body and her will standing between him and the growing menace of this destiny of memories that tore at him and claimed him for its own. "Love me!" she said.

And as she moved together with him in that ancient ritual of oneness he whispered, "I do love you...so damn much." And the snow continued to fall as they clung to each other for the entire night.

• • •

They settled down into a routine in which he worked at the reserve center, returned to the apartment where Stella would be waiting, eat supper with her and then just cuddle and talk, or listen to music until it was time for bed. He no longer mourned his mother, nor did he want to visit family members. He lived isolated in the cocoon of his own making, with a micro-family, which consisted of Stella and very slowly, some wounds healed.

He allowed himself the fantasy that he could survive Vietnam, return some day to Stella, and maybe marry—have children and rebuild a world that had been destroyed. Even though he knew that Vietnam was patiently waiting for him, he shoved it aside, and concentrated on loving this strange green-eyed girl who held him tight through the night and covered him with her soft body when he shivered uncontrollably or cried out in his sleep. He would wake up to find her kissing and holding him, impervious to the cold sweat, which always accompanied the dreams.

And then, one freezing morning, before he had to get ready for work, he felt her tears as they fell on his naked shoulder. Now it was his turn to comfort her, and he took her in his arms, holding her close and whispered, "Stella, what is it?"

"I don't want you to go back!" she whimpered.

He smiled, "It's not over until the fat lady sings my love. Maybe they'll let me stay."

"No." she said, "Your papers will come through, but you'll only get a

135

delay. In the end you'll have to go back."

He smiled and hugged her, "How could you possibly know that?"

"I have gypsy blood," she said, and he realized she was serious, "I sometimes see and know things. You'll go back and leave me."

Deciding to humor her, he asked, "and will I die, or be injured?'

She propped herself up on one elbow, "Tim, you're already dead inside. I feel a great emptiness inside which you cover with a thick shell that I can't break through and fill. Maybe no one will ever be able to reach you. I tried...I tried." She started crying again, so he held her closer.

"Don't worry so much," he said in an attempt to comfort her. "If they send me back I'll survive, I know how things work over there, what to do and when to do it. Besides, I have a lucky charm now, and it's you."

"I won't be like Linda, Tim," she said, "I won't promise to wait for you or even to love you if you return. The only thing we will ever have is today. Tomorrows are never certain and the past isn't worth remembering."

They fell silent, both staring at the ceiling, lost in thought. Then she propped herself up by her elbow and stroked his face. "If you come back, look for me and if you can't find me, find someone else who will love you with everything she's got, and maybe from time to time, think of me."

They lived every day as if it was their last. Both realized that time was running out and that his destiny was being determined by the indifferent clerks and bureaucrats that kept the meat-grinder that was the Vietnamese war functioning; and so they lost themselves in another world as she franticly tore at the shell that kept him safe from his memories.

Thanksgiving. The Reserve center closed down for the long weekend, and he politely declined several invitations from his mother's friends. Stella went home for thanksgiving dinner and Dennis brought his friend John to his father's farm for the celebration. He was alone in the apartment for most of the day, until he heard Stella open the door and walk in. He loved the way she smelled, fresh and crisp from the cold with a hint of her perfume that filled the room with a light of its own.

"God I hate thanksgiving with my step-dad." she said.

The visions of his own thanksgivings at home seeped into his thoughts and he pushed them away. "I'm thankful to be alive and that you're here with me. It's enough."

There is still one more thing I have to do," he said. "I have to go back one last time to the house where she died."

She hugged him for a moment, "Can I come with you?"

"Yes," he said. "I don't want to be alone. Pam gave me the key before she left town and I want to see the room where she died."

Stella nodded and held his hand as they walked down the stairs and into the VW bug.

The house was dark and lifeless. The lights still worked, and the heat was set at a minimum temperature to keep the water pipes from freezing. Everything was as he had left it. They walked into the room where she died, the room she had made ready for his return. Someone, probably Pam, had left his Smith Corona on the desk, and this time he determined to take it with him. He pictured her sitting at the desk and typing the rare letters he received from her while in Vietnam. He took the last letters he had received and placed them on the desktop.

"These were her last letters to me," he said, "and I wanted to sort of visualize her, sitting there, writing them."

"Can I see them?" Stella asked.

He handed her the letters. "Could you read them to me? I know it sounds crazy, but it would be like---I don't know—like a final good bye."

"Sure Tim." She said, and began to read in her soft voice.

"October 1

My Dear Son,

A letter from you at last – I'm proud of you for volunteering but terrible scared. Reports aren't very good coming out of that area and today it sounds even worse – (Sunday was bad enough!) I am happy you will be coming home soon but worried that you extended for another tour in that terrible war. No matter. Hurry up and come home, is all I can say. I know you never met your step-dad; I married him after you shipped out for Vietnam. I guess it was the loneliness, and then after all those years, he came back to Dunkirk and we just picked up where we left off after WWII."

Stella paused, "I didn't know that they had been...whatever. Did she ever mention him?"

"No. The first time I heard about him is just before I shipped out when she and I talked on the phone and she asked if I would have any objections if she married an old friend of hers that turned up out of the past. I wish I had said no." she held his hand and continued reading.

"He lost his job at the airbase for drinking and we got him a job down at the U.S. Rubber company. He is trying to pull himself together, not so ashamed anymore – etc. I feel so sorry for him, because he is so remorseful – and sometimes like a little boy saying, "What am I going to do! I should be in Vietnam fighting – instead of those young men." Etc. etc.

Anyway this is just a note to tell you how much I love you, miss you and pray for you and your buddies – we are 100% behind all of you, if that means anything – despite the junk you may read in the papers, etc. You are fighting a nastier war than WWII or even Korea – and doing a fine, fine job – Glad they are finally letting the B-52 bombers loose –gives you guys some advantages that you didn't have before.

The roses you had sent out to me from someone were beautiful, Tim and I was so touched and proud to get them. I can do so little for you now – Maybe both your step dad and I can get jobs in Saigon (Construction for him and secretarial for me) who knows!

Pam, your stepsister, has a job at Central Colony, after some very fine screening of the candidates. She will be working with retarded children. She will start off at the same pay I am getting now. More later, Love you always, Mom

Stella carefully refolded the letter and returned it to the envelope. She picked up the second letter and looked up as if asking permission to continue reading.

He nodded, swallowed the lump in his throat, and said, "Go ahead."

October 19

I got your letter saying you will be home before the end of the month. I am so excited. I set your room up and we're going to have a big welcome home party. I have another surprise for you—it looks like maybe we can really be a family again."

"Oh God!" a tear ran down her cheek and splashed on the letter. She placed the open letter on the table and wiped her eyes.

"Go on." he said.

Her hand trembled slightly as she picked the letter up. Her tear had caused the ink to blur.

We heard in the news that another bunch of Marines were killed – ambushed today – and, of course, you know the jitters I got – it's been so long now since you've been home – seems like a different world – and I miss you so very much. Wisconsin (UW) had another riot again but be assured it was instigated by the bunch of students from the East – the long beards and long hair – dirty unkempt b----'--.

And while they were demonstrating violently against the fact that Dow Chemical was still making napalm, more young men like you guys were being killed – ambushed – I'm proud to say though that only a handful of local students were involved.

Monday is your step-dad's birthday – he will be 45 – it will probably be a down in the mouth one for him-sans loosing driver's license for drunken driving, losing the good job at the airport job, and etc. – but now at least the only way he has left to go is "up." I am sure when you get home you can set things right. Well, must close for now, but had to get a letter off to you – makes me feel closer to you somehow, even if I have nothing much to report. Love always, Mom

She folded the letter and handed it back. They sat together in silence for a while; sheltering one another from the emptiness of the room until finally she turned to him and said, "Tim, there's something I have to tell you."

"Not now, Stella. Not now." And he took the typewriter, put it back in its case, and led her out of that house of death and back to the apartment where the living forgot about the dead in their celebration of life.

It was right after that Thanksgiving Weekend that the Gunny called him into the office. Seeing his expectant look the Gunny said, "No, sorry to disappoint you Brad, but the orders still haven't arrived. We expect them sometime this week though. However we do have a special assignment for you."

He was curious, "What assignment?"

"Well, since you are fresh back from Vietnam and the Old man's best friends with the Naval ROTC instructor, they thought you might want to address the class on Vietnam from the viewpoint of a combat NCO. Some of these guys will opt for the Marines when they graduate and the old man thought that getting a talk from someone who's been there might give them an edge. Will you do it?"

"I can say anything I want...I mean tell it like it is?"

"Yep, the Old Man wouldn't have it any other way and neither would I."

He smiled, "In that case, I'd be happy to."

"Ok. Uniform of the day, wintergreens, ribbons, and your expert rifleman badge. We want them to see a real marine. Take the rest of the day off, square away your uniform and report back to me at 1300. I'll drive you to the ROTC building, introduce you, and when you're done drive you back."

He made a quick trip to the farm, but Dennis told him that Stella wasn't there, so he continued to the apartment. She wasn't at the apartment either. He sighed and took the freshly laundered and pressed winter uniform out of its plastic bag and dressed in front of the mirror. He left a note saying he'd be back late, and drove back to the Reserve Center.

The Gunny gave him a quick once over and nodded in approval. "You ready for this, Brad?"

"I guess so. I'm not much for speaking in front of groups, but I'll do my best."

It was a short drive to the ROTC building, which was located on the other side of the campus, not far from the Army Math Research Center. Walking into the lecture room, he noticed that there were less people than he had expected. The commander introduced him, and the Gunny left him at the podium and took a seat near the back. "Let me introduce a Corporal, recently back from Vietnam. We've asked him to share his experience, in his own words, and then to be available for questions." They shook hands, and he was as alone as he would have been if he were walking point man back in the 'Nam.

D. RAMATI

He rested his hands on the podium and took a long look at the audience. Some were older than he was, but to his way of thinking, they were all just kids. Clearing his throat, he started his improvised lecture. "I spent some time here on the campus and almost joined the ROTC. I understand that you are both the Army and also Navy ROTC candidates, so what I have to say is only intended to reflect what I have experienced during my tour in Vietnam with the Marines. I won't be talking about either the Army or Navy, and am focusing entirely on what we saw in the Marines, and just in the I Corps. Does anyone know what the I Corps is?"

Silence.

"It is that part of Vietnam which extends from about Danang north to the North Vietnamese border, from the South China Sea West to Laos and Cambodia. The main enemy is not the VC for Vietcong, but the regular North Vietnamese Army. We call them Victor Charley and NVA. Do any of you intend to go into the regular service after you finish your ROTC? Can I see hands?"

He waited. Only two or three raised their hands, the others maintained a respectful silence.

"Ok, as far as I know if you stay in the Reserves you probably won't be called up, at least not for a while. You guy's in the back who raised your hands may want to think long and hard about going regular before you jump in. Ok, to get started; everything you are learning here does not, in any way apply to fighting in Vietnam. The war in Vietnam is fought mostly by small units sent out on search and destroy missions. Most of the action is at the company, platoon, or even fire team level. Your best friends are going to be close air support, artillery, and the availability of medivac helicopters. If you get commissioned and end up in Vietnam the first thing you have to learn is to shut your mouth and learn from your noncommissioned officers, who have been there, know the rules, and will save your ass from making mistakes that will get the men under your command killed. We don't take prisoners and neither do they. The only value a prisoner has to us is short time Intel quickly wrung out of him, and then we turn him into a good VC.

A new officer is about as worthless as tits on a boar when he's green

141

and only worth something if he survives his first 3 months in country. In the winter, all you have is rain, and the cold and wet sinks in until you never get warm. The summer is heat, dust, and constant thirst. There is NO rear area.

The VC is working with the NVA and acts as their eyes, ears, and more or less like their militia. They work in the fields and seem to live a normal life, but in truth, you can never know when the farmer, or a young boy, even a pretty girl will open up on you.

The areas are booby-trapped, especially the rice paddies, with submerged punji stakes, sharpened bamboo usually coated with shit. You'll be walking on a dyke between two paddies and they open up on you, and when you jump into the paddy, you land on the stakes. In other places, they have traps where you step into a small hole and your foot gets spiked from both sides, leaving you trapped. In the forest any manner of hidden cross bows, tree trunks, or anti personal mines are cleverly planted...so you need a real good experienced point man to clear the way...no one runs in Vietnam...every step could be your last.

The most feared is the Bouncing Betty. If you walk on it, you hear a click...and when you remove your foot it bounces up and hits you in the crotch...say good-bye to your balls and a good part of your legs. I remember one of our guys stepped on one and heard the click. We wrapped flak jackets around him, tied a rope around his waist, and pulled as hard as we could. It didn't work. He bled to death before we could medivac him.

Never let your men salute you, and never salute anyone. Never wear rank insignia. Their snipers are excellent. They always go for officers, NCOs, radiomen, corpsmen, and machine gunners first. Don't let your medics put that big Red Cross on their helmets or uniforms and for God's sake give them a weapon. Ours are issued 0.45 Cal. pistols. The Medic is the most important member of your command and after him, the radioman, and forward observers.

I know this sounds more like giving pointers rather than a lecture, but that's the picture of what's going on over there. There is NO big picture for the grunts on the ground, you don't even know where you're at most of the time, you use your section maps and only know the tactical objective you've been assigned.

The worst is the nights. Most of the time you are on 50% alert during the night, which means half the unit stays awake while the other half catches a few zzz's...slang for sleep. Don't ask me if we are winning the war because I don't have any idea, and after you've been in country for a week or so you won't give a shit. The only object is to stay alive, and keep the guys in your unit alive for as long as possible, and to kill as many of those rice propelled slope-heads as you can. And remember, we have a saying, 'little dink grow into big Cong'.

He paused and looked at the faces. He was in enemy territory. So he sighed and said, "Any questions?"

"We're getting a lot of flak from people here at the University. From what I hear from you some of the things they are saying might be true."

"Is that a question?" he asked, "No don't bother answering. I visited the Rat and saw what's happening. The enemy has no problem with giving a 10-year-old kid an AK-47 or an RPG and sending him to kill you. Just as there are no rear areas in Vietnam, there are no non-combatants, or at least you have to convince yourself of that. You hesitate at the wrong time and you'll get blown away or you'll be responsible for your friend going home in a body bag. I hate it too, but there is no clean way to fight a war."

"So what do you think should be done?" The question came from someone in the first row.

"I can only answer that the way it was explained to me from my Platoon Sergeant as we shipped out. He said don't get involved in a bar-room brawl if you aren't willing to get hurt and hurt people back."

"Are you going back?" he had been waiting for that question.

"I'm a Marine. I go where they send me. I do what they tell me for my corps and for my country. We have a saying 'Semper fidelity or Semper Fi for short' and it's the code we live by. From what I've seen here since my return, maybe going back isn't such a bad thing. Life is simpler there— you fight or die with your brothers, and we leave the moral judgments to people like you and to history. I volunteered for another tour because I wanted an assignment to the CAP (combined action program). It is supposed to help us win the hearts and minds of the Vietnamese by living in their villages, training them, giving medical aid, and when needed, help them defend their hamlets. From what I see, we might win the hearts and minds of the Vietnamese but we are losing the hearts and minds of the folks back home, especially here in the comfort of the universities. Are there any more questions?"

There were none and while a few bothered to shake his hand; most simply walked away. He walked to the car with the Gunny. "Was it worth it?" he asked.

"You mean the talk you gave?"

"Yeah."

"Don't know, but it was needed. The old Man'll be happy. You gave them a hell of a lot to think about. Let' get back, report in, and then grab a bite to eat before you go home."

Back at the Reserve center, they knocked on the Colonel's door and walked in when he said "Enter."

"Mission accomplished, Sir." The Gunny said.

"I heard. Just got off the phone with their commander. He said you were blunt, talked straight from the shoulder, and probably scared the shit out of some of them."

"I did my best, Sir." he said.

The colonel picked up some papers on his desk. "While you were having fun over at the University your orders came in."

He waited for the Colonel to go on. The next few words would change his life forever; what he would be, what he could become, and whether he would live or die.

In those few seconds, he thought about Stella. Would she wait for him? Did he love her...or was he even capable of love. No matter what his officer's next words would be, he knew she would leave him, and he would also leave behind a large part of what he had become in those few short days they shared.

"You'll be staying in the states—at least for the next two months. The Corps has decided you need a little time to recover and rebuild. They are sending you to Monterey California to brush up on your Vietnamese language and customs. They are transferring you to the language school and then back to Vietnam to the MACV Combined

Action Program as per your request when you extended your tour, but instead of the language training they normally give at PhuBai, you'll be going back to college and learning it from the experts. Do well and you should get promoted to Sergeant and be given command of a platoon working on the hearts and minds in the villages."

He waited in shocked silence, and just nodded.

"Your old unit will be regrouping and refitting in Okinawa. President Johnson hopes the war will be winding down after the next Christmas and Tet cease fire, so it's possible you might not be needed at all."

"Thank you, sir. When do I leave?"

"You'll be flying out of Truax on Sunday...so this is good bye and good luck." The Col. extended his hand and he took it. "Say your goodbye's and if you need anything before you ship out let me know."

And just like that, it was over. The Powers That Be in Marine Corps Headquarters had saved him from going back to Vietnam, but he knew it was only a reprieve; he would still have to pay the devil his dues and finish that second tour.

Before leaving the Reserve Center, he called Stella with the news. She said that she would be waiting at the apartment and from her voice; he could already tell she was anything but pleased. On the way back he reflected on how easy it was for The Powers to shuffle a little paper work and without knowing, or caring, change the direction of so many lives, his own included. They were giving him a little more time and he was grateful for every day, and while worried about returning to the mud, dust, and hardships of Vietnam, there was an appeal in being able at least to do something meaningful. The CAP program could supply that purpose. Monterey California and something called the a DLI (Defense Language Institute) program would give him time to get ready for his new assignment that would place him in PhuBai sometime in January 1968 just after the TET truce which was a mutual cease fire that had been holding for several years in honor of the Chinese New Year.

Stella was there when he walked into their apartment. Before he could say a word, she preempted him and said, "Why do you have to do this? Haven't you done enough for your precious Marine Corps?" She was angry and seemed a little desperate.

He didn't answer, then turned to her and said, "The Corps is all I have left now, Stella, and at least it is offering me two months of life before I go back"

"You could have had me," she whispered. Then she hesitated and added, "at least for now."

"No promises?" he asked.

"No promises," she said and then after a short pause added, "It's better that way." And as he looked into her eyes, he knew that she wouldn't be there when he got back. "I need distance, Tim. This is getting too serious for me. I can't just wake up one morning and watch you leave on your way back to Vietnam, and even if you come back alive, I won't sit around and wait for you. We could have maybe had a chance if you were ready to go to Canada, but you won't, so just drop me back at the farm." It was then that he noticed her backpack and suitcase behind the bed.

He held her for a while, and she kissed him then they left for the car. He carried her suitcase and she her backpack over one shoulder. They sat in silence. He drove into the dirt road leading to the old farmhouse. Both Dennis and John were waiting for them. Somewhat sheepishly, John took the suitcase from him and followed her into the house. Stella never looked back. Dennis stayed outside with him, and finally said, "I told you Tim. Stella's a free spirit," then, seeing the hurt, he added, "and sometimes she can be a mean bitch."

"She was going to tell me something, but I didn't let her. Do you know what she wanted to say?"

Dennis nodded. "She really didn't want to tell you until after you were gone. She almost told you when you had her read your mothers' letters to you—yes, she told me about that. She knows exactly what happened the night your mother was killed. She promised herself not to tell you until she knows for sure you are gone and beyond doing anything foolish. She wouldn't even tell me, but I'll make her write you when she feels she can talk about it. You have another week before the new renters move in to the apartment and normally you could stay here, but considering that Stella needs her distance, please don't ask me."

146

"I won't have to. My orders came in; I'll be flying out to the coast on Sunday." he said.

"I was sorry to hear that when Stella told me, but everything is Karma, Tim. Keep in touch, pick up the phone, and call us before you leave again for Vietnam. You can write her at this address and I'll make her write you back, but don't count on a lot of letters. Stella is.... Stella." he smiled apologetically.

They shook hands and as he drove back to the main road he saw Dennis waive him a gentle goodbye in the rear view mirror. He already missed them, crazy as it seemed, but they were an important part of the group of people that held him together; Stella with her body and Dennis with his unconditional friendship.

He made his rounds of good-byes and stored some of his personal effects taken from the house at his uncle's. On Sunday his uncle drove him to the airport in the VW and it was almost like that first time, except then Linda had been with them waving him good by as he boarded the plane. Now it was just the two of them, and as a parting gift, he gave his uncle the keys to the VW and told him to get the registration signed over in his name. There wasn't much that they ever said to each other, but the final admonishment was, "Tim...remember, live one day at a time. I'll see you when you come back for good."

He was in uniform and as he walked down the aisle in the Coach section there was none of the hostility he had felt back on the Campus, just people mildly interested, as they looked at yet another young man in uniform traveling to an unknown destination.

In Chicago, he changed planes for the West Coast and the hostility started. First, the Hare Krishna urged him to desert, and then a group of anti-war protestors cornered him in an attempt to convince him to refuse his orders. By that time, he was so tired he didn't argue with them and pushing the aggressive one out of his way, walked to the boarding area. There were others in uniform sitting there, waiting to debark for LA International, and together they formed a silent and isolated wall. They were a group apart from the others, of no interest to some, and an object of pity to others. If there were anti-war protestors among the passengers, they were wise enough to remain silent.

A DESTINY OF MEMORIES

As the plane lifted off he looked down at Chicago, and already the memories of his return from Vietnam came flooding back. He pulled down the shade and drifted into a troubled sleep. In his dreams, Linda morphed into Stella and back again and then into a whore he had used in Bangkok, then back into a young Vietnamese VC girl soldier he had executed and finally back to Stella again. He woke several times, and returned to his troubled dreams.

Finally the Stewardess woke him and told him they were descending and to fasten his seat belt. He looked out the window and saw the late afternoon anthill that is Los Angeles sprawling endlessly beneath him as the plane made its final approach.

Only one more connection, he told himself, and he'd be in Monterey.

He had heard of the Monterey International Pop Festival and was looking forward to visiting the place where the careers of so many rock stars had started. Songs that spoke to him in an entirely different way than the songs that sent him to Vietnam, like Good Vibrations and the Beach Boys' top hits, The Stones, Satisfaction, and Nancy Sinatra.

These new songs were by Jimi Hendrix, Janis Joplin, and Otis Redding, and different songs by Simon and Garfunkel, the Mamas and the Papas, the Who, the Byrds, Hugh Masekela, and Ravi Shankar. These songs were part of another generation, people like Stella and Dennis...he felt very old in thinking that a year and a half could be now called a generation as the momentum of time and change seemed to sweep all things into memories.

From his English Lit classes he remembered that Steinbeck immortalized Monterey in his novels Cannery Row, Tortilla Flat, and East of Eden. He wanted to visit the places mentioned in Steinbeck's books. When he arrived the first thing he did was to report in to the Presido Army language school which was located on a bluff with a fantastic view of Monterey Bay, and they informed him that his visions of touring Monterey were soon smashed with the announcement that he would begin orientation at 0800 the next morning.

He was ushered into "Marine Territory" which was a squad bay reserved for Marine NCO's and set apart from the others. Their rooms were basically small cubicles with partitions allowing each NCO a little privacy, a place for a footlocker, and a wall locker for his dress uniforms.

He took an empty cubical next to another Corporal who introduced himself as Lou Sage, also going back to CAP for a second tour. The others were preparing for their first tour in Vietnam and he and Lou quickly learned that they held a certain celebrity status. Lou explained to him that in addition to their classroom duties the Marine detachment would also do additional training and familiarization with their specific duties with the Combined Action Program on the weekends. Little if any time would be allotted for "shore leave."

"They do have a fairly good NCO club." Lou said by way of invitation, and they spent some hours that evening drinking beer and checking out the club. The club was inhabited by candidates from all three branches, Army, Navy, and Marines, which had a tendency to group together in various areas of the club. After a few beers, they headed back to the squad room and 'hit the rack for some Zzzz's.'

The next day found them in a classroom on the second floor of a new building located near enough to the ocean to give them a chance to breathe the fresh salt air. December was cold at night, but during the day, the temperatures warmed up considerably, and he found it a pleasant change from the sub-zero climate of Wisconsin in the winter.

The class commander was a senior Staff Sergeant. The ribbons on his chest were a roadmap that demanded respect. It clearly showed his two tours in Vietnam and that he had been awarded a silver star.

"Good morning Gentlemen." he said sardonically, "And welcome to your new home for the next 8 weeks. My name is Staff Sergeant Jones, you are the Marine contingent at this school, and the Corps expects you to outshine all the others. If you disappoint me may God have mercy on you because neither the corps nor I will have any. I see that two of you have spent time in Vietnam: Sage and Bratvold. Stand up let me see you."

They stood up.

"Ok," he said as he gave them a quick once over. "You two will stay after this orientation and will be squad leaders until the end of the course. Each evening, before lights out, you will report to me on the progress of your squads. There are 16 marines in the class excluding yourselves, and each one of you will be responsible for 8. First order of business: The uniform of the day will be starched and pressed utilities. Your weekends will be spent in additional training, including time at the rifle range, tactical instruction, and familiarization with the intricacies of the Combined Action Program. The classroom language instruction will be up to 16 hours a day including time for homework. I expect you to be courteous to your instructors and learn as much as you can in the relatively short period of time you'll be with us. Are there questions?"

In the back, someone asked about liberty on the weekends. The Staff Sergeant smiled, "Liberty? Oh, I almost forgot. You get one day off for Christmas and one 48-hour liberty to 'do the town' once a month. Upon graduation, you will have a 24-hour pass before you ship out to your overseas destinations. Any other stupid questions?" There were no more questions. "Ok then, let's get started."

The Staff Sergeant gave them the general history of the language program, explaining how the day would be broken into nine 55-minute sessions, with some of the classes being in a special language lab located on the campus. Their mornings would begin at 0600, calisthenics, cleaning up their squad bay and breakfast in the mess hall. They would report in to the class no later than 0800. They were given an hour break for lunch at 1200 and resume studies at 1300 until whatever time their instructors decided the day was done. Evening chow would be at 1900 in the mess hall and then they would be expected to pair up in the squad bay and practice. The slop chute (NCO Bar) would be off limits to them during the week. Navy PX privileges on Sunday if they were not doing a field exercise. It seemed to him that he wouldn't have much time to dwell on home and Stella.

Their instructors were Native Vietnamese speakers who either had been raised in the US or had been imported from Vietnam under a special agreement with the ARVN. Some had actually served with Marines in the CAP teams and they were a well of welcome information.

The mornings would cover practical Vietnamese in which two students would speak to each other following a dialog they had memorized the preceding night. They would learn military terms for useful things like hand grenade (shouliudan).

After lunch, they learned Vietnamese history and culture, customs, food, festivals and religions. This was followed by intensive language drill in the language labs where they were required to listen to Vietnamese words and sentences and repeat them, all of which was recorded and corrected by yet another Vietnamese instructor.

He wrote a short letter to Stella during that first week and sent it to the farm using Dennis' address. He bitterly remembered the unanswered letters he had sent to Linda, and steeled himself for the expected result of not getting an answering letter from Stella.

He was surprised that during mail call in the second week of the course, he did receive a letter, but it was only from Dennis. It said, '*Stella isn't living here, she left with somebody who was going out to San Francisco to join a band. If I hear from her, I will give her your address. Just keep on keeping on. Dennis*

He crumpled the letter and threw it away. San Francisco was only 100 miles away.

Lou commented, "You don't get many letters from home, Brad."

He looked at Lou, "that's because there isn't anyone back there in Wisconsin that knows how to write." he joked, but the joke sounded sour even to his own ears.

Lou wisely let the matter drop.

The friendly competition between his and Lou's squads brought them up to peak efficiency, and he was actually surprised how much of the language and culture they were absorbing in the short period, which was allowed.

Christmas day came. He was alone in the squad bay with Lou, who was Jewish and didn't observe Christmas, and a few other Marines who lived too far away to get home during the time permitted. The California Marines, who lived close by, offered to take them home for Christmas and for the most part everyone agreed. He had too many memories about Christmas to take up the offer, and Lou wasn't particularly interested, so they both stayed on the base for Christmas and rotated as duty NCOs relieving Staff Sergeant Jones, who took leave to be with his family in San Francisco.

Except for a visit to the NCO club, which held an informal Christmas party for those unfortunate enough to remain on base, the holiday passed with being haunted by visions of Christmas past...like Scrooge with thoughts of what might have been. That year the day after Christmas was the first day of Hanukkah and Lou made him go down to the Jewish center in town to join him with the lighting of the first candle of the eight-day celebration.

"You know," Lou said, "we observed Hanukah differently in the 'Nam."

"Ok," he answered, "I'll bite."

"Well," Lou drawled, "on the first day we went down to the village and burned one house. We burned two houses the next day and so on...on the last day we burned the entire village."

"Semper fi!" he raised his glass.

"Semper fi!" Lew answered and they touched their glasses, and downed the Jack Daniels in honor of the holiday.

Their graduation coincided with a new North Vietnamese offensive at dawn on the first day of the Tet holiday truce, Viet Cong forces--supported by large numbers of North Vietnamese troops--launch the largest and best-coordinated offensive of the war, driving into the center of South Vietnam's seven largest cities and attacking 30 provincial capitals from the Delta to the DMZ. Time seemed to stop for the next two weeks, with everyone being glued to the television, which showed some of the most furious fighting yet experienced in the war. There were no plans for a new course and the weeks were spent in a form of limbo known as "hurry up and wait."

Among the cities taken during the first four days of the offensive were Hue, Dalat, Kontum, and Quang Tri; in the north, all five provincial capitals were overrun. At the same time, enemy forces shelled numerous Allied airfields and bases. In Saigon, a 19-man Viet Cong suicide squad seized the U.S. Embassy and held it for six hours until an assault force of U.S. paratroopers landed by helicopter on the building's roof and routed them. Nearly 1,000 Viet Cong were believed to have infiltrated Saigon,

Their squads were sent to a staging battalion, for preparation for their first tour of Vietnam, which left the two of them without any orders and little to do in the empty squad-bay. Finally, they were called in to Sergeant Jones' office and were surprised to see a Marine Lieutenant Colonel waiting for them.

"Sit down please," he said. The Staff sergeant left the room leaving them alone with the Colonel. "My name is Colonel Hunt," he began, "and I suppose you are wondering about your orders?" the Colonel paused not expecting an answer then continued, "On the night of January 31, 1968, an estimated seventy-thousand communist soldiers launched a surprise attack into more than a hundred cities and towns of South Vietnam. It was monumentally successful. CAP platoons were overrun and the Marines slaughtered trying to defend their hamlets." Another paused to let it sink in.

"Everyone, Sir?" he asked.

"Over 90% were killed, usually tortured if they survived the first attack, and their heads mounted on pikes next to the village elders to show the villagers the price of collaboration. Essentially the Combined Action Marines were wiped out."

He and Lou exchanged glances but said nothing.

"We thought we could win the hearts and minds of the people. Well, that's over now, and this is why we need experienced Marines like you. We have established a new doctrine. In order to fight the VC and NVA we need to get to their level by becoming guerillas ourselves. This is our mobile doctrine, which will allow us to fight independently, you will carry all the gear you and your platoons will need to set up ambushes on the approaches to the hamlet. You will never return to a previous ambush site more than once and keep your platoon movements as unpredictable as possible. You will be working closely with an organization we refer to as "Phoenix." Are either of you familiar with the term?"

They looked at each other and both answered, "No Sir."

"Well, time enough for that later. We still believe in "hearts and minds," the colonel said, "but now it is a bit different. We give it to them here," he pointed to his heart, "and here." he pointed to his head, "but this time it will be bullets. Am I clear?"

There was no other answer so they replied, "Yes sir."

This operation will be handled completely with noncoms in tactical control. By the way, you both are now Sergeants. Congratulations. You will be shipping out from here to Iwo Kuni airbase in Japan and from there to Phu Bai to build your Platoons from scratch, using volunteer Marines and local ARVN's. Are there any questions?"

They knew the expected answer and so said in unisons, "No sir."

"Outstanding! So good luck and good hunting," he shook their hands, "take the evening off. You will be leaving on Military transport at 0800 tomorrow morning"

"So what now?" Lou asked as they left the room.

"Let's pack our gear go to town and get drunk and laid if possible."

"Sounds like a plan, Brad." Lou said with a gleam in his eye.

They picked up their orders, and were told to be ready to leave at 0600 for the El Toro airfield.

"We are going have one hell of a hangover." he remarked.

"It's a long flight to Japan, Brad, we can sleep it off." Lou answered.

They went to town and entered a waterfront bar. They were playing popular music and an occasional country and western tune. The girls were available, but the first order of business was drinking. They each ordered a pitcher of beer, steamed clams on the half shell, and a half a dozen crabs.

After a few more pitchers of beer and a boilermaker or two he got unsteadily to his feet, "I'm going to make a call."

"Thought you didn't know anyone who knew how to write." Lou joked.

"This is a call. They still speak English of sorts." he answered.

The pay phone was a small booth in the corner that allowed some privacy. He dialed Dennis' number at the farm. The phone rang about ten times before someone picked it up. It was Dennis.

"Hi Dennis, I'll be leaving for Vietnam tomorrow."

There was silence at the other end and then Dennis answered, "Just live it one day at a time. I'll see you when you get back Tim...oh, and I just got Stella's phone number. She is in San Francisco. Would you like to call her?"

He hesitated before answering. Did he want to call her or would it be

D. RAMATI

better just to forget. In the end he said, "Sure. Thanks. Why not?" He wrote the number down. At least, he told himself, it wouldn't be a long distance call.

When he called, someone picked the phone up right away, "Who is this?"

"Can I speak to Stella?" he asked.

"Who is this?"

"Just tell her it's Tim," he said. He heard some music in the background and someone called Stella to the phone. "It's someone called Tim. You wanna take the call?"

She picked up the phone, "Tim? How did you get this number?"

"From Dennis." he answered.

"Damn," she said, "I told him to keep it to himself. Well, damage's already done. What do you want?"

"I'm shipping out for Vietnam tomorrow, Stella." he said.

There was a sharp intake of breath, "You know that you don't have to go. If you run now we can hide you and then there's always Canada."

"I know," he said, "but there's something I have to finish."

"Even if it finishes us?" She asked.

"Even so." he answered.

"Then I guess this is a final goodbye."

"I wouldn't expect you to wait, Stella, but if I get back I would like to see you again."

"I have a new guy now, Tim. He plays in a band and we're living together. Anything can happen between now and then. Let's just say goodbye and let Karma take over." she sounded tired.

"But you were going to tell me something about my Mother." he said.

"I have written everything down and I am sending it to Dennis. If you get back, Dennis will give it to you. I saw everything go down that night and I didn't want to tell you because I don't want to be forced to talk about it at an inquest...I left it alone, and let Karma take over. Live, Tim, and read the letter when you get back and if it is meant to be, you'll find me or someone better than I am. I'm going to hang up now, don't bother to call back, we won't answer the phone until we know you have left." She hung up.

He walked back to the table, Lou had already attracted two girls, and they were drinking and laughing.

"You make your call?" Lou asked.

He nodded.

This is Julie and this is Sandi." Lou said.

He looked at the two California girls and there was a beach boy's song playing on the jukebox. "Excuse me," he said, "I need to walk the beach for a while to clear my head."

He got up and left them in the bar. It was still light outside, but evening was quickly approaching. He walked to the shore and looked into the West. The chariot of the sun was sinking below the horizon, being pulled by the grateful dead, who were calling to him.

As he turned and looked back at America it seemed as if a great darkness was covering the land, hiding all the horror he felt at his return, and he knew he probably wouldn't live to see either Dennis or Stella again, while behind him, the Chariot of the sun brought another new dawn to Vietnam the voices seemed to say that they would never leave or betray him...the voices of the grateful dead.

As he turned his back on America, there on that January shore where he stopped running from his memories he felt he had been totally and utterly—betrayed.

Letting his eyes follow the chariot of the Sun pulled by the Grateful dead as it sank beneath the Pacific horizon he knew he would keep on keeping on and that this would never the be the end...

ABOUT THE AUTHOR

D. Ramati served in the Marine Corps for two combat tours in Vietnam, where he received the Presidential Unit Citation. After an honorable discharge, he returned to complete his studies at the University of Wisconsin-Madison. After a long period of soul searching. Ramati converted to Orthodox Judaism and immigrated to Israel.

Ramati served for another 25 years in the Israel Defense Force, rising to the rank of Captain of infantry. Among his last assignments for the IDF was gathering intelligence information for a special unit of Military Intelligence. He became proficient in Hebrew and conversant in Arabic.